MANAGEMENT ANALYSIS IN PUBLIC ORGANIZATIONS

Management Analysis in Public Organizations

HISTORY, CONCEPTS, AND TECHNIQUES

Ray C. Oman, Stephen L. Damours,
T. Arthur Smith, and
Andrew R. Uscher

Foreword by
DAVID S. BROWN

Q

QUORUM BOOKS
New York • Westport, Connecticut • London

Library of Congress Cataloging-in-Publication Data

Management analysis in public organizations : history, concepts, and
  techniques / Ray Oman ... [et al.] ; foreword by David S. Brown.
      p. cm.
   Includes bibliographical references and index.
   ISBN 0-89930-403-6 (alk. paper)
   1. Organizational change. 2. Organizational effectiveness.
3. Public administration. I. Oman, Ray.
JF1525.073M35 1992
350.007—dc20   91-25533

British Library Cataloguing in Publication Data is available.

Library of Congress Catalog Card Number: 91-25533
ISBN: 0-89930-403-6

First published in 1992

Quorum Books, One Madison Avenue, New York, NY 10010
An imprint of Greenwood Publishing Group, Inc.

Printed in the United States of America

The paper used in this book complies with the
Permanent Paper Standard issued by the National
Information Standards Organization (Z39.48–1984).

10 9 8 7 6 5 4 3 2 1

Contents

Figures and Tables

Foreword

As organizations grow larger and accordingly more complex, the need for management analysis and management analysts has become increasingly important to good management. While the profession—and it clearly is one—has been practiced in the United States and elsewhere for well over half a century, there have been no authoritative books on the subject. Now there is one.

Management Analysis in Public Organizations: History, Concepts, and Techniques provides a very useful guide to the theory and practice of the field, and it fills a void long overlooked. Dr. Oman and his associates are practitioners with considerable experience as well as adjunct teachers, so their book contains a variety of practical approaches as well as theoretical justifications for the assignments they undertake.

No one knows how dependent the large organization, particularly the large public organization, is on its management analysts (there are over 17,000 in the federal government alone), but the profession has evolved logically—and successfully—from the "organization and methods examiners" who first appeared in the Ministry of the Treasury in Great Britain in the early 1900s. It has since that time embraced and included specific approaches contributed by industrial engineers, performance budgeting, organization development, productivity measurement, program evaluation, and, more recently, total quality management (TQM). It gives appropriate emphasis to the use of computers from a management and analytical point of view. As a guide to the continuing need for organization improvement, the authors have filled a void in the structuring and operation of the large, modern organization. Their contribution will be welcomed by those who work with both professional employees and members of the public in providing the services that modern public administration requires. Clearly, this book advances the knowledge of the field and is a contribution long overdue.

David S. Brown

Acknowledgment

The authors express their appreciation to Robert C. Harmon, without whose editorial expertise this book would not have been completed. Dr. Harmon has wide experience as a professional in the federal government, including the Department of Defense. He served as a professor at Gallaudet University for nineteen years, and he has edited numerous educational publications.

Introduction

The decade of the 1980s was traumatic for many organizations in the United States. It was a turbulent decade for federal government organizations because of wide funding fluctuations and changes in definitions of the proper role for government. Major cutbacks were made in most federal civilian agencies in the early 1980s. Many of these cutbacks extended as well to state and local governments, which received funding from their federal counterpart. At the same time the defense agencies were required to absorb and manage large budget increases that turned to budget reductions in a few short years. These new directions in funding were the result of changes in the view held by elected officials and the public at large concerning the proper role of government.

In the private sector as well, the 1980s were a time of major changes and the emergence of new trends. The growth in sales by foreign firms in the U.S. domestic market reached new highs. Many domestic firms saw their traditional markets shrink as foreign competition forced them to reassess their internal management and strategic relations. A feeling emerged that the United States may have lost its competitive edge, and there has been a frantic search for a way to regain momentum.

During much of the past decade the public sector turned to the private sector in its search for organizational and managerial "excellence," while the private sector turned abroad, notably to Japan. Many government organizations have sought to apply private-sector notions of competition, user fees, and privatization. Meanwhile, in private firms

Japanese approaches are the current fad in management training and executive development.

During the 1980s the faint awareness that our organizations were not as healthy as they should be or performing as well as they should grew into an acknowledged problem that had to be handled. Indeed, the inklings that something was wrong became an explicit concern, and the topic of conversation at business lunches as individual thoughts became shared concerns. It is now commonly accepted that the U.S. economy and organizations in the public and private sectors must search for new ways of doing business. This understanding has led to a plethora of publications in the professional and popular media designed to answer nagging questions about how to improve our management and organizations.

The surge of interest in ways to make organizations more competitive, efficient, and effective has come from many quarters and has taken many forms. Some of the key terms that appear to focus our ideas on organization improvement are *excellence*, *quality*, and *productivity*. Techniques that can serve as tools to improve our organizations run the gamut from *organization development* to productivity measurement and economic analysis. Some techniques that have recently basked in popularity include *managing for excellence*, *quality circles*, *customer-centered management*, and capital investment for productivity improvement. Approaches range from the "touchy feely" to "bean counting" and quantitative analysis.

An article by John A. Byrne in *Business Week* (January 20, 1986, pp. 52–61) dealt with business fads and "what's in" and "what's out." Business's preoccupation with the management approach currently in vogue has ranged from "scientific management" and "operations research" following World War II through PERT charts and organization development to "theory Z" and quality circles today. Many organizations have sought to solve their problems through what amounts to the quick fix and the fad.

This book is based on the premise that the quick fix will not work this time, but rather that organizations must seek lasting solutions to their systemic problems. The reason that one business fad has given way to another in the decades since World War II is that minor crises arose and then passed. None of the particular approaches employed at any one point in time could make more than an incremental difference in an organization's performance. Yet, as the immediate crisis passed and the organization appeared to be on a sound footing again, there was no need for a more concerted, long-term effort to resolve problems. The problems confronting U.S. organizations now, however, are more serious than the relatively minor crises of the past few decades, and any approach that is to make a difference must be more focused and long term. To use a medical analogy, the patient is more seriously ill than in the recent past and the treatment and the convalescent period will need to be extended.

The symptoms appearing in many organizations today are indicative of problems that need to be solved if an organization is to survive and maintain its status-quo position, and even more certainly must be dealt with if the organization is to grow and expand. Just as medical treatment must conform to the illness, so the organizational solution must conform to the problem. Just as physical, emotional, and mental health are intertwined in the individual, so are the human and technical factors, the morale, and the production functions in organizations. As the astute patient, noticing symptoms of illness, first contacts a general practitioner, so the shrewd manager, aware of organizational problems, contacts the management analyst.

One of the characteristics of the Japanese approach to organizations is the collection and analysis of much information before any definite actions are taken. Frequently, much long-term study is conducted before any overt effort is made to achieve a particular goal. Good information and analysis help make for good decisions. Consequently, the approach suggested in this book is based on a management analysis that is grounded in collecting and analyzing data to solve organizational problems. Data, information, and opinions provide the baseline for the analyst to assess reality within the organization and in its external environment. This is the "task" orientation of management analysis.

Another attribute of Japanese decision making is the use of discussion to reach a consensus among major parts of the organization. This method involves a lengthy process in which many viewpoints are aired and in which no decision is made until there is widespread agreement among participants. Although in-depth study, information, and analysis are critical, for Japanese decision making the process is key to an organization's effectiveness. "Process" is the second concept embedded in management analysis. "Process" is essential to organizational maintenance, just as data gathering and analysis are key "task" functions. For organizations to be successful in the long run, both process and task activities must play a part.

Management analysis brings to organizations both a task orientation for getting the job done and a process orientation for maintaining a positive organization climate. Although process and task activities are separate dimensions, they can contribute to or detract from one another. For example, the facts and information that are aired in a group discussion bring an informed approach to a problem, just as the meeting itself helps to create a positive atmosphere in the organization.

This book discusses how management analysis can increase organization efficiency, effectiveness, and productivity. Management analysis, as distinct from the business fads we have all known over the past decade or two, has a history long enough for it to have grown from infancy to adulthood, having emerged as a separate organizational function shortly after World War II. The roots of management analysis, however, go back even further, to the "scientific management" movement before the turn of the century. The field of management analysis has seen fads come and go, and it has incorporated the best of each into the fabric of the field. Management analysis is as broad as it is long in that it encompasses elements of quantitative scientific management as well as organization development and quality circles.

Administrators, managers, or owners of firms concerned with improving the overall effectiveness, efficiency, quality, and productivity of their organizations can benefit from this book. This book is also designed for supervisors of units that provide analytical support to operational and line managers, and above all for the analysts and evaluators who carry out management improvement efforts, be they formal studies or process interventions. Last, but not least, administrative and management assistants, administrative officers, and others who perform management improvement efforts on an occasional or part-time basis should gain from the book.

The book is written for the hard-headed manager or analyst who is interested in balancing the forces of productivity, positive working climate, and personal survival in his or her organization. The manager or analyst who views success in terms of years rather than months will get much out of this book as will the organization actor who recognizes both the facade and substance of what happens in organizations, but who believes that substance in the long run will more often determine success or failure.

CHAPTER 1 _____

Management Analysis Defined: Dilemmas and Opportunities in Organizations

U.S. organizations face many dilemmas as well as opportunities over the next decade. As discussed in the introduction, these dilemmas relate to problems of resource scarcity, such as tight budgets for many government agencies; increased competition for many private firms because of foreign competition; and a rapidly changing, even turbulent environment, brought on by poor management, obsolescence, and sectoral and regional changes. If organizations are to be successful and "hold their own," an even, balanced, and longer-term approach, based on sound management and organization principles, is necessary.

These trying times will call on the full range of managers' talents dealing with the gamut of classic management functions proposed by thinkers such as Henri Fayol[1] and Luther Gulick,[2] including planning, organizing, directing, staffing, coordinating, reviewing, and budgeting (PODSCORB).[3] Although Henry Mintzberg in his book, *The Nature of Managerial Work*,[4] has characterized management in terms different from those of classic PODSCORB functions, citing the fragmentation and wide variety of the work, the role of managers in making decisions to run organizations is, if anything, accentuated. If one were to single out one aspect of a manager's job that could be thought of as most important, it would be decision making.

One of the characteristics of successful organizations is the ability to make good decisions. Decisions are key to organizational success because they establish the direction of the organization. Once a decision is made, the organization must live with it for a period of time. Further, decisions often provide the basis for the allocation of resources. A sound decision will benefit the organization, while a poor decision will result in a net cost.

Good information and analysis are the basis for sound decisions that produce a net benefit for the organization. The impact of the quality of decisions on organizations will be seen both in the short run and the long run. Although organizations may have been able to tolerate seat-of-the-pants management in the past, the pressures now are such that muddling through is a luxury they can no longer afford. In the present highly competitive climate, organizations must optimize decision making by using the best information and analysis available.

Management analysis (MA), or "analysis for management," can contribute to many aspects of organization decision making and, in particular, to all of the processes suggested by management thinkers from Fayol to Mintzberg. MA assists the manager/decision maker by providing information and analysis. Although information and analysis are useful during all phases of the management processes, they are especially valuable at decision points when the classic management analysis study can make a particular contribution to sound decision making.

With its roots in the scientific management movement of the late nineteenth century and the organization and methods examiners who emerged in the Ministry of the Treasury in Great Britain shortly after the turn of the century, MA has grown to include the full range of management techniques over the past forty years.[5] MA is now in a position to make a major contribution to organizations as they prepare to compete, survive, and grow during the 1990s.

Here are some examples of the kinds of questions that management analysts can help answer.

1. What kind of an organization to design to perform assigned functions;
2. What approach to use to assess the performance of an ongoing program;
3. Which kind of computer system to acquire to carry out the management's intent to implement an MIS (management information system);
4. What kind of productivity measurement system to develop to meet organization needs;
5. What kind of MIS to design to meet the needs of organization managers and decision makers;
6. What organization structure to develop to facilitate achieving top management's objectives;
7. What type of office automation system to acquire to provide better administrative and clerical support;
8. What actions to take to implement an organization-wide quality improvement initiative;

9. How to streamline the work process and procedures in a procurement operation;

10. How to design and implement an organizationwide cost-cutting effort;

11. What actions to take in improving organization effectiveness; and

12. How to improve the quality of work life in the organization.

This list is merely suggestive of the kinds of questions addressed in MA.

MANAGEMENT ANALYSIS: PRESENT AND PAST

Honora B. Peter wrote in the *Washington Post*:

In his column of July 22, Mike Causey mentions that somewhere or other, there is an opening for a GS-11 management analyst. This revives a question that has always plagued me: What is a management analyst and what does he do? In the thirty-two years I worked for the Federal government, I was never able to figure this one out.

Of course, periodically a mandate for some report or other exuded from their bunkhouse for which we had to take time out to fabricate answers. But, we seldom heard any more about the results of a compilation of our fabrications, unless it was an announcement at long last that the report was no longer required.

That is why the hiring of "management consultants" from the so-called "beltway bandits" befuddled me even more. Oh well, no consultant was ever hired to do more than tell the hirer that he was already doing a great job.[6]

Questions like that expressed in this article are often raised about analytical staff jobs in areas such as management analysis, program analysis, economic analysis, and operations research. Nevertheless, there are thousands of management analysts in federal, state, and local government as well as in private industry.

Many organizations employ individuals whose job is to analyze management and organization problems, develop recommendations, and implement solutions. The problems they deal with typically fall into the two general categories: operating efficiency and program effectiveness. The solution or amelioration of an organization problem, or to put it in a positive frame, the improvement of organization efficiency and effectiveness, usually involves a change in an output or a change in the process by which an output is produced. If there is to be an improvement, the relevant individuals must change so that the process by which the output is created, or the output itself, is altered.

THE FIELD OF
MANAGEMENT ANALYSIS

MA is one of several occupational series in the federal government concerned with providing analytical support for managers and decision makers. Other occupational series that provide this kind of expertise are program analysis, industrial engineering, operations research analysis, economic analysis, and sometimes budget analysis. Of these series, management analysis and program analysis are the largest with over 17,000 and 21,000 personnel, respectively. There are 12,000 budget analysts, 6,000 economists, and a smaller number of operations research analysts and industrial engineers.[7] MA can be distinguished from other analytical job series by its size, its focus on management issues, and the wide distribution of management analysts throughout the federal government. There are also many thousands of management analysts in state, county, and municipal governments, and a number of associations and private corporations also have management analysis functions.

An indication of the dynamism of the field is the growth in the number of management analysts in the federal government. Between 1987 and 1989, for example, the number of analysts grew from 15,694 to 17,265, an increase of 10 percent. Over the decade from 1980 to 1989 the number of management analysts has grown by over 6,100 for a 55 percent increase.[8] The growth is significant considering that over the past twenty years the total number of federal government employees has remained static or declined slightly. Another trend has been that women constitute a growing proportion of the field. Although the reasons for the expansion of the field are not entirely clear, organizations' needs for analysis related to management is clearly a factor. Another contributing factor has been the use of management analysts in high-growth areas in the government, such as information resource management, computers, and quality and productivity. Interestingly, the number of program analysts has also grown rapidly during this period.

As a staff function, MA provides support to managers at various levels about organization and management questions. The Office of Personnel Management (OPM) Classification Standards state that:

The Management Analysis occupation rests on the concept that certain functions and responsibilities to managers are susceptible to analysis and improvement by specialists who are experts in these functions, in the principles that underlie their administration, and in the techniques of their analysis.[9]

OPM Qualification Standards note that:

1. providing advice and conducting studies concerning management and organization;
2. developing and conducting programs aimed at stimulating management improvement throughout the agency; and
3. performing developmental or operating work to apply specialized management tools or techniques such as automatic data processing (ADP) planning, work measurement, and organization control.[22]

An examination of the functional statements for a sample of fifteen MA units[23] in another research effort indicated the following major responsibilities and activities:

1. to plan, develop, and conduct a comprehensive program of management support and consultative services;
2. to conduct major studies and surveys to improve systems, operations, management effectiveness, control, performance, productivity, efficiency, and economy;
3. to assure the appropriate documentation of policy and procedures through a directives management system;
4. to provide liaison for external audits;
5. to review and evaluate organization action proposals;
6. to conduct organization and staffing surveys, studies, and reviews.

Major functions and responsibilities mentioned by heads of management analysis units included responsibility for the following:

- organization structure
- delegations of authority
- records and reports management
- management advice
- privacy act
- office systems
- manpower allocation
- micrographics
- resource allocation for the budget process
- monitor consulting service contracts.

An examination of recent job announcements for management analysts indicates a demand for analysts with expertise in strategic planning, total quality management (TQM), work measurement, productivity, and automation and information systems.

INTERVIEWS WITH MANAGEMENT ANALYSIS OFFICERS

Interviews with the heads of MA units provide an interesting perspective of the field. The following information was collected in personal interviews with MA officers.[24] One interviewee had a number of aphorisms for describing MA and the management analysts. They included:

"Management analysis requires a love of puzzles."

"Management analysts are loners."

"Good management analysis requires creative interpretation."

"It is not enough to be factually correct if people don't use it."

"Being a management analyst requires complete intellectual freedom."

"A management analyst needs an environment where he can say and think what he wants, where he does not have to change his opinion."

"Management analysts do not necessarily work well with each other, but must be able to work with people outside in the larger organization."

"Analysts must be able to interpret the meanings of what people say."

Not all the heads of MA units were as articulate in describing management analysis, yet each was interested in discussing the field.

The division chief interviewed above noted that his approach to MA was largely grounded in the behavioral sciences. Other MA officers interviewed had different orientations to the field. Some analysts, for example, see themselves as providing objective, third-party perspectives based on hard facts. This perspective emphasizes the use of facts and objective data-gathering rather than the use of political or behavioral skills.

One of the department-level MA units interviewed had a sizable staff of between thirty and forty professionals. Managing such a large staff had given the unit head exposure to many kinds of management analysts and management studies. His perceptions of MA are reflected in the following statements:

"Management analysis is the application of common sense."

"Management analysts tend to be perfectionists."

"Management analysts like to give the perfect solution to problems, sometimes ignoring the law of diminishing returns on effort expended."

"Management analysts are academically oriented."

MA was defined as "the science of examining a problem or issue, real or perceived, breaking it into component parts, and applying common sense to the solution."

The MA officer related a story about meeting with a top decision maker in which management analysts were deep in discussion about defining a problem and proposing alternative solutions. The top decision maker, annoyed with the amount of time and energy devoted to thinking through the problem and solution, stated, "You think on your own time, but you work on mine."

ORGANIZATIONAL DISTRIBUTION OF MANAGEMENT ANALYSTS

Separate organization units devoted to MA have spread throughout the civilian and defense sectors of the federal government in the past thirty-five years. Most of these units are located at the division level and are commonly known as "management and organization," "management analysis," "management systems," and "management consulting" divisions. MA units are usually small, having between five and ten analysts, although the authors are aware of a few large units that have between twenty and thirty analysts. Organizationally, many of these units are located under the administrative or administrative management arm of the agency.

All federal departments, nearly all bureaus, and many independent agencies have MA units. The U.S. Office of Personnel Management's Report on the Federal Civilian Workforce indicated there were nearly 17,300 management analysts in the federal government in 1989.[25] The distribution of management analysts for major agencies is shown in Table 1.1.

MANAGEMENT ANALYSIS IN PERSPECTIVE

Managers at all organization levels confront complex problems. These problems may have their genesis in human, technical, or procedural systems, or they may have other causes. Many organizations in both the public and private sectors employ specialists to help solve and ameliorate management and organization problems or to improve current operations. These specialists include external and internal management consultants, operations research analysts, organization development specialists, economists, program analysts, and management analysts. If a continuum were established extending from a rigorous, quantitative emphasis on the one hand to a focus on human problems with nonquantifiable factors on the other, operations research would be located at one extreme with organization development at the other. Management analysis would be located between these two extremes, and because of its multifaceted nature would occupy more than

Table 1.1
Distribution of Management Analysts in Major Agencies

Agency	Total Employment
Agriculture	569
Air Force	2,009
Army	5,276
Commerce	194
Other Defense	1,106
Justice	378
Labor	115
Education	210
Energy	211
Environmental Protection Agency	145
General Services Administration	144
Health and Human Services	925
Housing and Urban Development	236
Interior	202
National Aeronautics and Space Administration	78
Navy	2,717
State	83
Transportation	245
Treasury	1,424
Veterans Administration	473
Total for major agencies	16,740
Total for all federal agencies	17,265

Source: U.S. Office of Personnel Management

one segment on the continuum. Thus, MA is a subset of a larger group of specialists in problem solving.

The MA occupational series is distinguished from other staff analytical fields in the federal government in several respects. First, much of MA is based on broad principles of management and organization. For example, the notions of formal organization charts, functional statements, delegations of authority, span of control, and management processes and systems are fundamental to the MA field. These conceptual frameworks have general applicability to all organizations and are often shared by analysts of different agencies. Furthermore, management analysts are usually generalists, and their tools and techniques are as applicable to one organization as to another. Management analysts often have job mobility and can change from one organization to another more easily than can those in other fields.

Second, because in the federal government entry requirements into the MA field are general and do not specify a baccalaureate in a particular area, the job series is truly interdisciplinary. Analysts come from academic backgrounds as diverse as history, literature, philosophy, business administration, economics, and public administration. And although there is a common core of concepts, the field is defined in part by the climate of the particular organization where it is practiced. MA is designed to be responsive to the needs of management rather than to a particular discipline. The academic fields most closely related to MA are probably management science and public administration, and in the private sector, business administration. These fields are very interdisciplinary and integrative.

Despite their usual organization location together with other administrative units, MA functions are different from the others in a number of ways. For example, a large percentage of resources in most MA shops is used to conduct ad hoc studies. Analysts who perform these studies often have no line functions and in a sense exist as a slack resource to be employed on an as-needed basis to meet organization requirements. In addition, MA is often different from many other administrative management activities in that it does not perform as part of a larger system. Rather, it operates through the use of small interventions or studies.

Many administrative management functions, for example, are concerned with large systems or processes, such as the budget, personnel, or accounting. MA units, in large part, operate independently of large organization-wide systems. The work of the analyst is to analyze problems, propose solutions, and sometimes design systems, rather than to maintain large systems or perform routine activities.

To carry out their mission, MA units typically conduct special studies, advise on management questions, work on organization structure and functions, and write delegations of authority, administrative issuances, and directives. Conducting management studies is usually the most important and time-consuming activity. These studies are usually concerned with questions of economy, efficiency, effectiveness, work methods and procedures, and organization structure and functions. Many studies are of organization-wide issues commonly raised by mid-level or top-level management. Managers and decision makers are frequently involved in various aspects of the study and in the eventual review and approval of recommendations.

Analysts typically have an excellent overview of their own agency and often have well-informed views of other agencies because of their role in management studies and in external liaison and coordination. Although MA units are often located at the division level in bureaus, their influence in the informal organization frequently extends much higher. For example, the heads of MA units often serve as management consultants to top program and agency managers, thus having access to the highest level of power in an organization.

NOTES

1. Fayol, Henri, *General and Industrial Management*, trans. C. Storrs (London: Sir Isaac Pitman and Sons, 1949).

2. Gulick, Luther H., "Notes on the Theory of Organizations," in Luther Gulick and Lyndall Urwick, eds., *Papers on the Science of Administration* (New York: Columbia University Press, 1969).

3. Carroll, Stephen J., and Dennis J. Gillen, "Are the Classical Management Functions Useful in Describing Managerial Work," *Academy of Management Review* 12, no. 1 (1987): 38–51.

4. Mintzberg, Henry, *The Nature of Managerial Work* (New York: Harper & Row, 1973).

5. See Lyngseth, D. M., "The Use of Organization and Methods in Canadian Government," *Canadian Public Administration* 4, no. 4 (December 1962): 428–492; Melrose, E. D., "Organization and Methods," *Public Administration* 38 (Summer 1960): 119–130; and Pittman, I. J., "Organization and Methods," *Public Administration* 26 (1948): 1–9.

6. Peter, Honora B., "Those 'Management Analysts'," *Washington Post*, August 4, 1981, p. A-14.

7. U.S. Office of Personnel Management, Federation Occupation Survey as of September 30, 1989, Table J.

8. Interview on November 26, 1990, with Christine E. Steele of the U.S. Office of Personnel Management, Office of Workforce Information, Statistical Analysis and Services Division, pertaining to the number of management analysts shown in the records of occupations of federal white-collar and blue-collar workers.

9. U.S. Office of Personnel Management, *Position Classification Standards* TS9, February 1972, p. 3.

10. U.S. Office of Personnel Management, *Qualification Standards* TS141, February 1972, p. 1.

11. U.S. Office of Management and Budget, *Bulletin No. 78–12*, April 1978.

12. U.S. Office of Personnel Management, *Qualifications Standards* TS141, February 1972, p. 1. The U.S. Office of Personnel Management published a new standard titled, *Position-Classification Standard for Management and Program Analysis Series*, GS-343, TS-98, August 1990. This new guide contains standards for establishing grade levels for management and program positions and is based on the old standards for management analysis. It has not yet been implemented in most agencies.

13. Brown, David S., "The Management Analyst: Who is He and What Does

He Do?" Department of Public Administration, George Washington University, Washington, D.C., p. 1.

14. Ibid., p. 1.

15. Afzal, Mohammad, "Management Analysis: An Emerging Staff Function," unpublished doctoral dissertation, Cornell University, Ithaca, N.Y., June 1962, p. 127.

16. Ibid., p. 122.

17. Rapp, William F., "Management Analysis at the Headquarters of Federal Agencies," *International Review of Administrative Sciences* 26, no. 3, 1960, p. 1.

18. U.S. Office of Personnel Management, Federal Occupation Survey as of September 30, 1989, Table J.

19. U.S. Bureau of the Budget, "Management Analysis at the Headquarters of Federal Agencies: An Inventory of Agency Practices Concerning the Staff Function of Management Analysis," October 1959, p. 8.

20. Ibid., p. 13.

21. Rapp, 1960, p. 236.

22. Ibid., p. 238.

23. Oman, Ray C., and LTC Sam L. Lyles, "Management Analysis in the Federal Government," *Armed Forces Comptroller* 28, no. 4 (Fall 1983): 15.

24. Oman, Ray C., "The Nature, Conduct, and Acceptance of Management Analysis Studies in Civilian Federal Agencies," unpublished doctoral dissertation, The George Washington University, Washington, D.C., 1983, pp. 63–64.

25. U.S. Office of Personnel Management, Federal Occupation Survey as of September 30, 1989, Table J.

CHAPTER 2 _____

Management Analysis Studies:
An Overview

As discussed in the Introduction and Chapter 1, organizations in almost all sectors of U.S. society are confronting a difficult and often turbulent environment. Organizations are being challenged today as they have not been in the recent past. The period of almost continual growth and expansion that we knew in much of the 1960s and 1970s has obviously ended, and new and stiffer challenges abide in almost all quarters. For private firms this challenge comes largely in the form of increased foreign competition, while for public organizations it takes the form of static or declining budget resources.

The time has come when, if organizations are truly to compete, they must seek real solutions to the real severe problems they confront. No longer will the business fads referred to in a recent article be sufficient to solve the problems many organizations face.[1] The key to resolving organizational problems lies in intelligent decision making. The twin factors of good information and good analysis are essential to sound decision making. While these factors in themselves do not assure sound decisions, they increase the probability of good decision making and ensure better performance over a period of time.

Management analysis (MA) is uniquely able to provide good information and good analysis to organization managers confronting difficult decisions. It does this by focusing on the value of information and analysis and on the organization's decision-making and implementation processes. Having grown and matured in the United States over the past forty years, MA embraces a wide variety of approaches and techniques that can improve organization effectiveness, efficiency, quality, and productivity.

Table 2.1
Models of Decision Making

Rational Comprehensive Model	Successive Limited Comparisons Model
1. Clarification of values or objectives is distinct from and usually before analysis of alternative policies.	1. Value goals and analysis of the action alternatives are closely intertwined.
2. Policy-formulation is therefore approached through means-end analysis: First the ends are agreed upon, then the means to achieve them are sought.	2. Since means and ends are not distinct, means-end analysis is often inappropriate or limited.
3. The test of a "good" policy is that it can be shown to be the most appropriate means to a given end.	3. The test of "good" policy is that various analysts find themselves agreeing on an alternative course of action (without their agreeing that it is the most appropriate means to an agreed upon objective).

4. Analysis is comprehensive; every important relevant factor is taken into account.	4. Analysis is drastically limited;
	
	  i. Important possible outcomes are neglected.
	
	  ii. Important alternative potential policies are neglected.
	
	  iii. Important affected values are neglected.

5. Theory is usually heavily relied upon.	5. A succession of comparisons greatly reduces or eliminates reliance on theory.

Adapted from Charles Lindblom, "The Science of Muddling Through," *Public Administration Review* 19, no. 2 (Spring 1959): 79–88.

These approaches include the quantitative and the qualitative, the objective and the subjective, and the "hard nosed" and the "touchy-feely." The approach taken by management analysts is related to two commonly used decision-making models in public administration: the rational comprehensive model and the incremental model. The good management analyst is comfortable working with either of these approaches. Table 2.1 depicts the major elements of these two different models of decision making.[2]

Our discussion of how MA can help organizations to be more efficient, effective, and productive will start with decision making, one of the most important functions in organizations. It is here that the tool typically associated with MA, the study, is characteristically applied. The decision-making process usually arises because a problem or opportunity has been identified and a decision must be made on a course of action. In the process of making a decision, there will be an opportunity for the presentation of ideas, beliefs, opinions, alternatives, information, and analysis. Formal studies or analyses are frequently, although not necessarily, part of the decision-making process.

MAKING DECISIONS IN ORGANIZATIONS

Making decisions is an important part of the job of most senior managers, policymakers, or organization officials. Decisions are made, of course, by personnel at all levels. Most of the personnel, however, make decisions on a day-to-day basis that are operational in nature and usually made within the framework of existing policies and guidelines. Decisions involving the expenditure of considerable resources, whether dollars, personnel, or time, are normally reserved for managers, policymakers, or other senior officials. These are the decisions in which the organization has a sizable investment at stake.

The nature of decision making varies, of course, with the organization and its environment. In some organizations, decision making is decentralized and junior personnel have considerable authority,[3] while in others it may reside only at the top of the organizational hierarchy.[4] In some cases, decision-making authority may be concentrated in one or two parts of the organizations, finance and budget for example, while in others it may be more dispersed. Further, the number and importance of decisions made may vary through time. During times of rapid change either within the organization or the environment, as in times of great expansion or contraction, for example, many decisions may have to be made in a short period of time.

The forum in which decisions are made can vary considerably, of course, depending on the nature of the organization and the management style of its key actors. In some organizations decisions are apt to be made in a more open environment, while in others they will be made behind closed doors. In more democratic and participative organizations, decisions are likely to be made after considerable consultation, perhaps within the context of a meeting. In authoritarian organizations with highly centralized power structures, decisions are apt to be made in a more "close hold" fashion with the final word emanating from the office of the senior official.

Two types of situations require a decision: (1) When there is a problem that entails finding and taking the correct course of action and (2) When there is an opportunity for improvement if we can find and take appropriate measures. Since decisions involve the commitment of organization resources and assets, most policymakers believe the expenditure of considerable time and effort to reach good decisions is well worth it even if the result is nothing more than turning a marginally bad decision into a marginally good one. Much of the decision-making process consists of gathering and analyzing information. Considerable time and effort may also be spent in the "soul searching," discussion, and debate that are part of the process itself.

Management studies are frequently key to providing information and analysis to assist in or improve decision making. Such studies provide information and analysis and evaluate alternative courses of action or decisions. Decision makers often request formal studies to assist in making the best decision. Formal studies can range from the so-called "quicky" study to major efforts conducted over a considerable period of time. Studies usually result in written reports, although oral briefings or presentations frequently are used to supplement the written product.

MANAGEMENT ANALYSIS STUDIES—
PAST AND PRESENT

The 1958 Bureau of the Budget study found that although management analysts have many functions, management studies and analyses form the core and most unifying element in the field.[5] The BOB survey of twenty-five management analysis units at agency headquarters found that management studies were conducted in 88 percent of the units contacted. Other functions carried out in more than half of the MA units were directives management, management promotion, and organization control. The study also found that the top five activities in terms of professional staff time were management studies, automatic data processing (ADP) planning, directives management, management promotion, and organization control. About three times as much effort was spent on management studies as on the next largest activity. The studies were classified into four basic types: general management surveys, organization studies, systems and procedures studies, and special studies. Heads of management analysis units pointed out that analysts' work was principally in the form of studies.[6]

As part of the BOB study, heads of MA units expressed their views about management studies:

1. It is necessary to be selective in accepting studies because of the large amount of time they take.
2. Top level executives directly or indirectly initiated a large share of the studies.

3. Many requests for studies also came from operating elements and other staff and service groups.

4. Fewer studies were initiated by MA groups themselves than by other groups.

5. Studies that heads of MA units wanted to conduct often had to be given low priority because of other urgent, specific problems.

6. Most MA units avoided initiating studies that would affect specific organizational units without first securing the concurrence of concerned officials.

7. Several units reported an effort to avoid studies of a particularly extensive and sweeping nature because experience had shown that events overtake long-term studies.

8. Many studies by MA units were conducted jointly with personnel from program or other staff elements.

9. A common policy was to conduct studies in such close cooperation with the units concerned that the recommendations would be in effect prior to the completion of the formal report.

10. It was felt that the team approach, which blended various experiences and skills, provided better recommendations on complex problems.[7]

The BOB study also noted some comments pertaining to study methodology from heads of MA shops at the headquarters of agencies. For example:

There is no general effort to develop an objective discipline in the conduct of studies or to use more powerful tools of investigation and analysis; a few staffs, however, had added personnel with particular qualifications in statistics or management science.[8]

Although management analysts are involved every year in hundreds of studies to improve decision making and to alter management practices, a search of the literature has revealed little information about the kinds of topics studied or the methods used to conduct the studies. Salaries alone for the 17,000 management analysts in the federal government totaled over $600 million in 1989.[9] While not all management analysts are engaged primarily in studies, studies frequently involve interdisciplinary and interunit teams representing various parts of the organization and often demand considerable time from top management, personnel who provide information, and others not directly involved in the study. When these factors are considered, MA studies in the federal government alone certainly cost well over $1 billion annually. Thus, management analyses represent a rich and untapped source of information about studies.

Our research on MA studies is based on the information collected from management analysts and decision makers in fifteen randomly selected agencies.[10] MA units were selected by a stratified random sample of the seventy-three units present in the twelve cabinet-level civilian departments and three independent agencies. One MA unit was selected per agency. The fifteen units chosen, therefore, make up a sample of approximately 20 percent. Only units with five or more analysts were included in the sampling frame.

In conducting our analysis of MA studies, first, more-general information was gathered from interviews with heads of these MA units and from organization function statements. Then, a particular study that had been conducted to assist in decision making was selected for detailed examination (see Chapters 4 and 8).

Most of the heads of MA units indicated that studies were their most important activity. Studies were sometimes an important aspect of carrying out other activities. One MA officer identified the following major activities of his unit: organization studies; manpower allocation; management advice, often in the form of consulting services; and traditional MA studies. Another MA unit head felt his two most important functions were working on budget and resource allocation questions and special studies. He indicated that many of the studies dealt with questions about how to keep the budget down and how to "do more with less."

The kinds of studies frequently mentioned in interviews included organization structure, workload, productivity, word processing and office automation, work measurement studies, benefit/cost, and procedures and processes. A review of the functional statements for the fifteen randomly selected management analysis units revealed the following kinds of studies:

1. studies of agency methods, procedures, workflow, staffing, and organization;

2. analytical, quantitative management studies using mathematical, statistical, and operations research tools;

3. organization and staffing surveys, studies, and reviews; and

4. management studies for the development of decision-making information and establishment of management systems to improve efficiency, effectiveness, and economy, and to delineate missions and functional responsibilities and improve organizational relationships.

Chapter 4 gives a description of the fifteen large MA studies examined including an assessment of the methods and processes used, while Chapter 8 discusses decision makers' acceptance of study recommendations.

NOTES

1. Byrne, John A., "Business Fads: What's In—What's Out," *Business Week* (January 20, 1986): 52–61.

2. Lindblom, Charles, "The Science of Muddling Through," *Public Administration Review* 19, no. 2 (Spring 1959): 79–88.

3. Weber, Max, *The Theory of Social and Economic Organization* (New York: Free Press, 1964).

4. Silverman, David, *The Theory of Organizations* (New York: Basic Books, 1971).

5. Rapp, William F., "Management Analysis at the Headquarters of Federal Agencies," *International Review of Administrative Sciences* 26, no. 3 (1960).

6. Ibid., pp. 244–245.

7. Ibid., pp. 237–239.

8. Ibid., p. 244.

9. The U.S. Office of Personnel Management, Federal Occupation Survey as of September 30, 1989, Table C 1 indicated the average salary for management analysts including the 3.6 percent pay raise effective January 1, 1990, was $37,000. The average pay for program analysts according to the same source was $43,900.

10. Oman, Ray C., "The Nature, Conduct, and Acceptance of Management Analysis Studies in Civilian Federal Agencies," unpublished doctoral dissertation, The George Washington University, Washington, D.C., 1983.

CHAPTER 3 _____

Organizational Structure: The Skeleton

In the work of management analysts, one function is almost always present: dealing with issues of organizational structure. Documenting structures and functions of organizations, studying structures and recommending alternatives, and guiding and facilitating the process of organizational change are all among the most traditional and pervasive functions of management analysts. This chapter looks at organizational structure as something that is always present, whether consciously or not, in human cooperation and particularly in management. It then looks at the management analyst's role and contribution as a potentially valuable element in the frequent upheavals and structural changes in large organizations. The chapter concludes by surveying some of the diversity of structural principles or patterns that are found in large modern organizations. It speaks to the needed flexibility in the management analyst's approach in dealing with the variety of structuring principles.

THE BASIC PROBLEMS OF COOPERATION

When people work together cooperatively, they are inevitably confronted with a problem: who will do what work and who will make what kinds of decisions? The very act of working together implies that a prior problem has already been solved at least partially: agreement on a goal or objective. However, goals and objectives have a way of shifting over time as circumstances change and tend to recur as problems unless the project or cooperative effort is simple and short-lived.

The process of solving these basic problems of deciding what needs to be done and why, who will do which work, and who will guide or control the work process, is both politics and management analysis. The outcome is organizational structure at its most basic, the skeleton of any cooperative effort. The interpersonal and intergroup processes, the social and emotional dimension, are politics with a small *p*. The more systematic, rational part of the process is management analysis. Of course with small organizations or informal groups, this process of dividing up the work and the decision making tasks is often done by the seat of the pants without conscious thought of either politics or management analysis. Often, one person is a dominant personality or is elected to lead, and either makes the decisions about work allocation or structures the process of discussion by which the decisions are made. Even so, in successful organizations a degree of conscious thought and rationality enters into the process of dividing up the work and the decision making. This process is management analysis. It is always present, whether it is done by a management analyst or not. Management analysis in this sense is not an option but a necessity. The only question is how well it will be done.

In large organizations the problems of how to divide up the work and the decision-making authority become enormously complex and controversial and are rarely settled issues for long. Structural problems are frequently revisited and new decisions made. These decisions, once made, have profound effects, not only on the immediate ability of the organization to do the work or meet the challenge of a change in its environment, but more importantly on the future ability of the organization to make competent and adaptive decisions, to deal with new and unexpected problems. Organizational structure is a product of decision making, but also controls subsequent decision making. Suppose the advocate of a far-sighted point of view or the producer of a product with high potential usefulness in the future loses power in a reorganization by moving down in the hierarchy of authority. There are now more management layers above as an obstacle to this person's being heard or this product's being appreciated and supported by top management. The affected person or organizational unit is in a weaker position to influence the next major decisions, possibly to the detriment of the organization as a whole. The structure is itself the product of a decision or a series of decisions, and it affects future decisions.

ENTER THE MANAGEMENT ANALYST

The role of the management analyst in all this can be central and extremely valuable. The management analyst, or a person with another job title but essentially the same function, can contribute clear thinking in the confused and emotionally charged atmosphere of a reorganization and can simplify the complex problems of division of work and authority by bringing to bear a unique point of view and a unique set of skills. First, the analyst can offer the key decision maker a relatively disinterested, objective point of view in the midst of the excitement of line managers struggling for power and advocating the merits of their own organizations, products or services, and values.

Second, the analyst can bring to bear a well-established and experientially tested set of concepts and rules of thumb about what works and what does not work in organizational structures. These concepts will be explored later in this chapter. Despite numerous situational exceptions, there is a remarkably simple and reliable set of principles for organizational structuring that are widely known, but for political reasons in reorganizations, often honored more in the breach than in the observance. The analyst can apply these in developing alternative organizational structures or proposals for management to consider and can explore their relative merits using specific numerical indicators such as supervisory ratios. The management analyst can serve as a voice for these elements of sanity when the politics of reorganization move in directions that are dangerously irrational.

A third role of the management analyst, and one of the most valuable, is that of guide to structuring the discussion and decision-making processes that lead to a major reorganization. One model for decision-making processes, commonly used in traditionally managed organizations, is for a single top manager or a very small group of key people secretly to develop a reorganization plan they think will solve the organization's problems, or promote their own agenda for the future of the organization. The plan is then "leaked," sometimes accidentally but often deliberately, and the designers of the new structure have an opportunity to find out how the idea is received by the rest of the organization. This process can sometimes be unpleasant, especially when the reaction is extremely adverse, but the process (not the adverse reaction) has the advantage to the "in" group of giving them the most control of what happens. Before forcing implementation of the plan, they can be magnanimous and modify the plan as necessary to accommodate the concerns that surface as a result of the leak.

NOBODY KNOWS ENOUGH

In organizations of several thousand employees, such as are common in government and not unusual in business, no one single person, neither a line manager nor a management analyst, knows or understands all that the organization is doing or how it does it. The reality is far too complex for a single mind to encompass. Anyone who doubts this need only make a superficial start at understanding an organization by selecting a government agency or business bureaucracy at random and reading the functional statements of the various organizational units and the position descriptions of a few hundred positions in these units. The result of this exquisitely painful process is to suggest that the task of fully understanding the organization is at least daunting, if not hopeless. Anyone who has read or written position descriptions knows that for many jobs they are the merest shadow, the barest minimum of information about what the incumbent actually does, and to some degree they are deliberately misleading, designed to support the highest possible grade and therefore pay level for the job. Other sources of information, such as budget documents, are also bulky, sketchy, and misleading. The sheer quantity of information needed to understand a large organization defies capturing and presenting in any orderly fashion. Perhaps more important, there is an indeterminacy principle at work: if the organization can afford to invest much effort in documenting its internal structures and work processes in detail, the documentation is most likely there for a purpose: to acquire more resources or justify current levels, not to present an unbiased picture. The picture is biased roughly in proportion to the magnitude of the resources at stake, and the very existence of the self-made picture suggests that the creator has some axe to grind other than an aesthetic or scientific one.

THE SIMPLIFIERS

Managers and analysts often use organization charts, system flow diagrams, staffing ratios, and the like as well statements of the main functions and missions of organizations to document current structures and alternatives. These efforts can be extremely valuable, even critical to success. But the results are usually superficial; they often deal with the more obvious facts and not with the subtler aspects of the problem such as the social, cultural, motivational, or political dimensions. An organization is an organism, and it has analogues not only to the human muscular and skeletal and digestive systems, some of the more obvious factors in activity, but also analogues to the less obvious complexities of the endocrine system, the lymphatic system, the electrolyte balance, and so on. These subtleties could no doubt be charted if there were enough knowledge, but both the state of the art in charting and knowledge of how organizations work are not equal to the task.

KNOWING HOW TO TALK

Because of the information overload problem, in a complex, major reorganization only a well-ordered collective process in which a number of managers and staff people share information and jointly recommend decisions can lead to a well-informed and well-considered result. Such a result takes into account, often unconsciously, the subtler forces at work in an organization. A competent management analyst knows this and is ready to suggest to key line managers effective group processes for developing and discussing recommendations on organizational changes.

A large literature on organizational development has arisen over the past thirty years and provides innumerable examples of structured group processes for creating alternative problem solutions, discussing their merits, deciding among them, and exploring implementation issues. The most successful of these group processes have in common breaking down the creative and analytical tasks into several discrete steps, defining clearly to the group the step or steps they are to carry out, establishing rules of operation for the group that are vital to the specific step in the process, and then monitoring the group process to assure that the rules of operation are followed.

The most familiar example is brainstorming, where uninhibited creation of as many ideas as possible is the first goal, and where one of the most important rules is to refrain from criticizing ideas until a later stage in the process. Another example comes from the discipline of value analysis, where a group develops a cluster of criteria to use in evaluating alternative solutions to a problem and then applies the criteria systematically to each alternative, often assigning numerical scores expressing how each alternative stacks up against each criterion. For example, a particular proposed organizational structure might get a score of ten on a scale of ten for focusing management attention on a special project, but score only a five or a three on minimizing the total number of organizational units (and therefore supervisors) in the new structure. The scores of this alternative are later compared with the scores of others, and a decision is made on which alternative to recommend to the manager who has the final decision-making authority.

In all this, the management analyst must be familiar with various ways to chart or present alternative organizational structures and various ways to arrange discussions of these structures so as to elicit as much information as possible before management jumps to a decision. The essence of the management analyst's role is to advocate a well-designed discussion process and to adapt general knowledge of how to conduct these processes to the unique situations that arise in organizations. The analyst may know in advance which of several organizational alternatives is the best, but he or she would be wise not simply to tell management what to do, unless the alternatives are extremely simple and obvious or the managers unusually willing to be led. Managers at several levels in an organization must think out loud in the form of discussions and come to a decision for themselves, because later they will accept the decision as partly their own and will know why an alternative with greater advantages along certain lines was not selected. The resulting organizational structure will last longer and be better accepted, and morale after the reorganization will be much better among managers who had a chance to be heard.

BASIC STRUCTURAL PRINCIPLES

Almost everyone who has read anything about management has encountered the old "ho-hum" concepts of chain of command, span of control, authority and responsibility, line and staff, centralization and decentralization, and the like. However familiar sounding they may be, they remain some of the foundations of organizational structuring, and when they are ignored or improperly applied, the results are almost always unfortunate, if not disastrous. Despite repeated attacks and challenges by management theorists, they remain truisms that cannot be ignored. Having recognized their importance, we need also to recognize that the collective understanding of their meaning has gone through important changes, and that they must be applied in different ways in different situations. A manufacturing company, a professional association, and a research laboratory need radically different organizational structures. We also need to recognize that other factors besides the traditional formal hierarchy of authority are critical in structuring work processes in organizations. These include informal discussion and cooperation in teams and task forces and various types of standardization such as well-defined patterns of repetitive action in mass production, and qualification standards for selection of professional employees.

THE DURABLE CHAIN

"Chain of command" is always the most basic structural element. It is an amalgam of a metaphor, the reference to "chain" implying bondage and also a series of linkages, and a more literal concept, "command," the exercise of formal authority to tell someone else what to do. In the traditional view, orders are given from above in the chain of command, and those further down are obligated (bound by the chain) to carry them out. The obligation may stem from law, regulation, tradition, or ownership of key resources, but whatever the source of the authority to give orders, commands are formed by the superior in the chain and imposed on the subordinate. Reality, of course, is not so simple. In modern organizations, the directions on what to do often move up the chain rather than down, because the expertise on what to do and how to do it resides not with the manager but with subordinate specialists. They may have greater expertise in their specialized professional or technical field than the manager does. They formulate recommendations and pass them up the chain for ratification. In most instances the supervisor or manager approving the recommendation is in a position to place it in a larger context and see its broader implications more clearly than the subordinate specialist. But this same manager may not fully understand the detailed technical implications of the proposal or may have a partially faulty understanding. In some instances the manager has only a general understanding of complex technical issues and is forced by circumstances to trust the goodwill and expertise of subordinates. This is particularly true in systems that rotate managers, such as the military and the foreign service.

Who, then, is really in control? And which way is the command really moving? Expertise partially replaces formal authority as the controlling factor in decision making. Where expertise is critical, as it is in modern professional bureaucracies, a considerable share of decision making is decentralized. Nevertheless, a formal hierarchy of authority seems to be an operational necessity, even in the most highly knowledge-oriented organizations. There are always competing points of view about what should be done, how, and by whom, and how resources should be allocated. Someone must make the final decisions after hearing the arguments. This same person—the supervisor or manager, the person up the chain of command—must integrate political considerations, what the people still higher in the organization and various constituency groups (Congress, the board of directors, the owner of the company, or whatever) will accept.

The concept of chain of command has been repeatedly attacked and challenged, as such concepts should be, by management theorists who say that authority depends on the assent of those below the decision maker—that it moves up, not down, because of the assent of the governed and the authority of experts, and so on. Despite these challenges and useful modifications, the concept remains at the heart of organizational structuring in the real world; no large or mid-sized organization is without its hierarchy of authority. The governed may consent, but they are nevertheless governed. Expertise may go up, but decisions still come down. There may be town meetings, but there is also a mayor and a few town employees to carry out the decisions and make further, more-detailed implementing decisions.

HOW WIDE A SPAN?

How many people can one supervisor effectively direct? The question has been debated endlessly, and yet it must be answered time after

Figure 3.1
Normal Organization

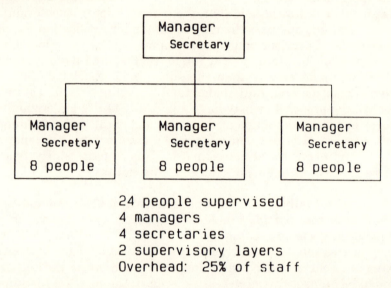

```
24 people supervised
4 managers
4 secretaries
2 supervisory layers
Overhead: 25% of staff
```

time in real-world decision making. The usual rule of thumb answer is three to ten. The real answer, of course, is "it all depends." An often overlooked essential principle is that the span of control should be as wide as possible, even to the point of appearing unreasonably wide, especially at the bottom of the hierarchy. For illustrations of the disasters that can happen in organizational structuring when this simple principle is neglected, see the illustrative organization charts in figures 3.1 through 3.3. More employees per supervisor at the bottom of the organization means fewer supervisors and fewer layers of supervision. Conversely, fewer employees per supervisor means more supervisors or layers of supervision to guide the same number of employees. The more layers of supervision there are between the top decision makers and the workers, the greater the difficulty in guiding the organization realistically and decisively. In the extremely layered organization given in the hypothetical example shown in the three organization charts, the top manager is far less likely to know what is going on at the working level than is the top manager of the "normal" organization. Information is filtered going up, and decisions are diluted and reinterpreted going down. And more people in management and supervision means more overhead.

It is realistic, not cynical, to say that in organizations with more than three layers of supervision, the loss of information going up and down the chain of command approximates 100 percent. In an informal experiment on this subject that one of the authors was privy to, the

Figure 3.2
Extremely Fragmented Organization

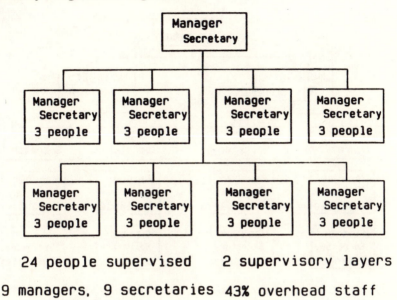

24 people supervised   2 supervisory layers

9 managers, 9 secretaries 43% overhead staff

top executive in a disciplined, well-managed organization of four layers directed his immediate subordinates, all high-level, extremely competent line managers, to pass a message down the chain of command and make sure it reached the section chief level. These managers were to pass the message to their division chiefs, who were in turn to pass it to their section chiefs. Two weeks later, all two hundred section chiefs were polled, and not one had received the message. So little information gets through, except in writing by direct mailing, that one can safely assume nothing will get through. A tall chain of command aggravates this problem.

Given, in most situations, the advantages of a wide span of control and a short chain of command, in other words, a relatively "flat" organization, why are narrow spans of control and tall chains of command so often found in organizations? What perverse impulse drives people to design and live with inefficient organizations? The short answer is the need to reward good performers (or the boss's friends) with higher salaries and supervisory responsibilities. As more people are moved up into the management ranks, more management positions have to be created and more organizations, or more layers, have to be created to provide a raison d'être for the positions. The most common abuse of organizational structure for this purpose is fragmentation, dividing the organization into more and more smaller organizations to create

Figure 3.3
Extremely Layered Organization

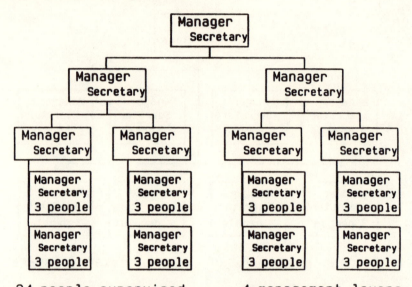

24 people supervised   4 management layers
15 managers, 15 secretaries   55.5% overhead positions

more first-line supervisor positions. While this widens the span of control of the layer of management immediately above the fragmented lower level, it means fewer employees to supervise for each first-line supervisor. The final result is more managers managing the same number of people. In other words, fragmentation costs money in salaries for unnecessary supervisors. Again, see the hypothetical organization charts for examples.

In addition to communication and efficiency, another key advantage of a wide span of control is morale. Numerous studies have shown that relative autonomy or independence of action correlate closely with high employee job satisfaction, and close supervision is associated with poor morale. The correlation between high morale and low turnover is obvious. Often, people need and want far less supervision than their superiors would like to believe, and they stay longer and learn to do their jobs better if they have greater freedom.

HOLDING THE LINE

Despite the advantages (in the abstract) of wide spans of control, when powerful line managers in an organization are determined to create middle-management jobs for their favorite employees and thereby produce a fragmented structure or additional layers, there is nothing even the best management analyst, operating in an advisory capacity, can do to stop them. The finger in the dike does not hold back a tidal wave.

But between reorganizations, when managers are in a state of relative mental clarity, a skillful management analyst can get often get them to agree in principle to the advantages of wide spans of control, short chains of command, and minimal fragmentation as general goals, and can establish written organizational policies on acceptable organizational structures. These policies, cited at appropriate moments, become norms the organization looks to during reorganizations. They also become, in effect, an institutionalized voice for rationality that will support and sustain the management analyst's consulting efforts to minimize the damage of political considerations in reorganizations. These policies can be further reinforced if controls or procedures are established that require that reorganization plans be reviewed for policy compliance before being approved by top management.

THE LAYERS ON THE CAKE

In designing an organization, it is always better to err in the direction of designing a wide, flat organization initially, and to fall back and introduce more layers if supervisors cannot cope and exercise appropriate control. Organizational layers are easy to create and all but impossible to eliminate. They become centers of power and vested interest that can be dislodged by only the most powerful, energetic, and ruthless top manager. But there are generic patterns of circumstances that make wider or narrower spans of control reasonable. The traditional three to ten people can be stretched far beyond the limits of theory if the circumstances are right. One person can supervise far more than ten when the subordinates are highly motivated, highly responsible, and disciplined people who know how to do their jobs so well they need little guidance. The classic example is the university president, who may supervise thirty people, including office directors and department chairpersons, people who can do their jobs without much supervision.

Additional factors affecting the breadth of the feasible span of control are:

1. the relative independence or interdependence of subordinates' work; the more interdependent, the more occasions there are for conflict or problems among subordinates and decision making by the supervisor;
2. the availability of experienced workers to guide the less experienced and thus serve as informal team leaders for purposes of technical guidance;

3. the frequency and intensity of large-scale external challenges and crises requiring centralized decision making and coordinated initiative to cope with the challenge;

4. the volume of the flow of information up the chain for approval or other formal action;

5. the need for consistency of policy interpretation in similar situations under the control of different employees (the more employees a manager must supervise, the more difficulty he or she may have monitoring and enforcing consistency); and

6. the diversity of work being done by subordinates: the more diverse, the more difficult to manage.

CENTRALIZATION AND DECENTRALIZATION

As with span of control, the arguments about the relative merits of centralization and decentralization are endless. So are the cycles of oscillation between these poles in many organizations. Again, to the question, "Which is better?" the answer is, it all depends. But what it depends on can be understood and defined. Surprisingly little rational and balanced discussion of this important subject is to be found in management literature. But the important broad outlines of the subject are almost intuitively obvious.

Centralized decision-making authority is essential in organizations where the main challenges confront the entire organization, not some subordinate part of it. If the challenges come fast, as they sometimes do to an army in wartime, there may be little time for participative decision making. In such a situation, centralized, authoritarian management works best because there is no other option that works at all. But in many large modern organizations, there are several product lines or services being produced, and different management challenges and requirements confront each of them. A degree of decentralization is essential for success, since a few executives in a central organization cannot know enough or process information fast enough on a wide enough variety of subjects to make timely and wise decisions for the whole organization.

The key principle is that decision-making authority must be at the organizational level, in the hands of the executive or group of executives, who are as close to the action as possible while still being able to make the things happen that they have decided on. The failure to act on this simple principle is the reason that highly centralized industrial organizations with in-depth expertise in one or a few product lines almost always fail when they try to play the conglomerate game and acquire an alien business. They strangle the newly acquired organization with controls and centralized decision-making processes that are inappropriate to its natural mode of successful operation. Harassed and inhibited in decision making, the newcomer company misses opportunities, responds inappropriately or too late to problems, and turns in big losses, thereby "proving" the incompetence of its executives and triggering still further centralization of decision making in the "wiser" hands of the new owner. The vicious cycle continues until eventually the owner, bled white by the losses of the subsidiary, sells it at yet another loss, and staggers on toward recovery or bankruptcy.

By contrast, a conglomerate or holding company that often acquires businesses as its own natural mode of operation may replace key executives in a new acquisition, but usually it keeps interference in the internal management and decision making to a minimum; in other words, it operates successfully on a radically decentralized basis. It links itself to the new subsidiary through finances but does not try to become an organizational Siamese twin with the newcomer. The result is that the subsidiary is at least not prevented from operating successfully and may turn in a profit.

ECONOMIES OF SCALE

The most basic principle to consider in deciding whether to centralize or decentralize parts of a large organization, especially administrative support functions such as human resources, accounting, and procurement and contracting, can be summed up in four words: effectiveness first, then efficiency. Centralizations of staff services in large organizations (with tens of thousands of employees), for instance, intended to produce economies of scale, almost never produce anything but inefficient and ineffective bureaucracies that satisfy no one. A large, centralized administrative support system is clumsy and slow by its very nature, and cannot respond quickly to the needs of its users. The hidden costs of slow, unresponsive service far outweigh the documented savings of such reorganizations. A large, cumbersome support system fails to provide adequate support and goes the way of the dinosaurs in the long run. It may take its parent organization with it when it goes.

The U.S. government runs this experiment over and over, every time an administration comes in that is more concerned about saving money than about delivering services. Various administrative support functions are consolidated from the bureau level to the departmental level. Units that served thousands of employees now serve tens of thousands or hundreds of thousands. The change is ballyhooed as a great savings to the taxpayer and a demonstration of the advantages of businesslike operation of the government. However, reality eventually sets in and managers have to live with the change after the initiator has been promoted to still dizzier heights of political glory. The departmental elephant thus created cannot dance nimbly enough to meet the needs of the bureaus. The result of the original centralization move is almost always the same: both poorer service delivery and higher costs. Eventually the frustration of managers at the bureau level who are trying to make the system work becomes intolerable, and the decision is made to return these services to their former, more-decentralized positions.

Most businesses that stand out as successful relative to others in the same industry do not operate highly centralized administrative support systems, if we are to believe the results of extensive research on successful companies in *The Search for Excellence*. These notably successful companies allow a maximum of latitude to local managers in order to secure their own services in the quickest and least expensive way they can. For the most part the parent company exercises only results-oriented controls on subordinate units. Government agencies cannot generally operate in this way, enmeshed as they are in intricate and expensive "cost-saving" regulations and procedures that have evolved over the years in response to political pressures and consequent legislation.

Government agencies can, however, resist the temptation of the mirage of economies of scale and locate administrative support operations in medium-sized units (usually bureaus, a few hundred to a few thousand employees) where they can be effective and responsive, rather than in the largest agencies (scores or hundreds of thousands of employees). While management analysts cannot stop politically motivated managers from taking drastic and destructive steps in organizational realignment such as radical centralizations for economies of scale, they can sound warnings if other highly placed managers are willing to listen, and they can work to minimize the damage in the short run and restore organizational effectiveness in the longer run. Fortunately for the government, management analysts as a group, and career employees in general, outlast political appointees.

TYPES OF ORGANIZATIONS

Until now in this discussion of management analysts and organizational structures, we have made only casual references to an important concept, namely the architectural dictum (somewhat dated now in the field of architecture, but still on target for our purposes): form follows function. Note that this is ideal, not necessarily real. Often enough, form gets in the way of function in buildings as well as organizations. Also, in buildings, form can be aesthetic or decorative; in organizations we can seldom afford that luxury. Alertness to different general types of functions and the ways they can be organized can help the management analyst guide managers away from current fads and their equally mindless opposite, hidebound traditions. Away from these toward what? Toward structures that facilitate whatever functions the organization needs to perform.

An excellent exploration of the subject of different organizational forms can be found in Henry Mintzberg's book *The Structuring of Organizations* (Prentice-Hall, 1979). Mintzberg offers, among other subjects, an illuminating typology of organizations based not so much on the specific details of what they do substantively as on how they structure themselves internally to meet the typical challenges they confront. Function here is broadly conceived: manufacturing, repetitive professional work (e.g., hospitals, schools), innovation, and so on. Mintzberg's typology is not based on specific functions and organizations built to perform them, but rather is a loose descriptive portrait of different types of organizations and how they are well or poorly adapted to a variety of functions. He identifies five broad types of organization.

The first is the simple structure, typically entrepreneurial, with one dominant leader, a short chain of command, a wide span of control, and little support staff; the key ability of the organization is quick reaction to opportunities and crises. Management analysts are seldom found in such organizations.

The second type is the "machine bureaucracy" that relies on standardized work processes, central authority lodged in the chain of command and in the technical personnel who standardize the work, and an environment that provides a relatively stable demand for the organization's product. The strength of the organization is predictability, efficiency, and control; its function is typically manufacturing something for which there is a steady demand. Management analysts and their close relatives, industrial engineers, often have influential roles in such organizations.

A third type is the professional bureaucracy, which delivers professional work to users such as university students, hospital patients, or the like. These organizations exist to deliver the services their operating cores provide, and because the professions provide quality standards, little supervision and standardization of work is necessary. They therefore have, typically, a wide span of control and little internal effort to standardize the work. Since standardization is done by the outside organizations of the profession, industrial engineers are likely to be absent. But management analysts or internal management consultants may be a part of the large administrative support systems these organizations develop to deliver services to the core professionals. These analysts assist with big-picture organizational questions, automation and streamlining of administrative support, and so on.

The fourth type of organization in Mintzberg's typology is the divisionalized form, the product-oriented organization with separate divisions for each product and each division with its own purchasing, engineering, manufacturing, and marketing capabilities. This organization is typically a cluster of machine bureaucracies or professional bureaucracies within a central organization that exercises central control by not micromanaging the divisions but by defining performance standards (e.g., profitability), and monitoring the results achieved or not achieved by the divisions. Examples include most of the Fortune 500 companies as well as the "multiversity" or university with several campuses, and hospital systems with specialized hospitals within them.

When an organization's basic work is innovation, it can no longer use the four more-traditional structures outlined above, and a fifth tends to emerge, called by Mintzberg and others the "ad hocracy." Generally it hires experts or professionals, but rather than putting them into well-defined roles where they use their professional expertise in predictable patterns, as doctors in a hospital or instructors in a university do, they are placed in units defined by function or academic discipline for administrative convenience and then combined with experts in other fields into project teams that do the creative work of the organization. This arrangement is the stimulating but difficult-to-manage matrix management system. It produces conflict and stress, but also unpredictable, creative results that are at the far opposite pole from the extremely standardized, predictable outputs of the machine bureaucracy. Research laboratories, space agencies, computer software companies, television networks, and other highly creative organizations in rapidly shifting environments use this structure, or unstructure, to stay limber enough to produce constantly new and different products.

SO WHAT?

The beginning or intermediate management analyst might most benefit from learning one important point from the brief coverage of a vast subject in this chapter. The message is a paradox: there are universal principles, and every situation is unique. The principles must be kept in mind, but always applied with sensitivity and creativity to the specific oddity of the situation. Doctrinaire application of the basic principles of formal hierarchy of authority, span of control, chain of command, delegation of authority, and the rest can result in organizational disasters, or, more likely, the irrelevance of the fusty, hidebound management analyst who is behind the state of the art from the outset. As the discussion of different types of organization highlights, these principles are applied radically differently in a machine bureaucracy, where they are all-important and all-controlling, and in an ad hocracy, where they are present but attenuated in the extreme, and often less important than informal teamwork.

CONCLUSION

Organizational changes are usually driven by management discomfort, a sense in the minds of key line managers that something is not right with the organization. While a structural change alone may provide a solution, more often reorganization is only a distraction if the cause of the problem is not well diagnosed. Quite often the real cause of the problem is not structural, or is only partly structural and is partly a result of other weaknesses or maladaptations to changes in the organization's environment. The task of diagnosing the organization's illness, its specific current problem(s), and finding solutions is another key function of the management analyst. The process of this diagnosis and prescription, called a management study, may result in procedural changes, policy changes, or programmatic changes, rather than or along with structural changes. In addition to organizational consulting, management studies are at the very heart of the management analyst's function.

CHAPTER 4 _____

An Analysis of a Sample of Large Management Analysis Studies

Not only is the role of the management analyst in improving organizations a rich source of information, but the studies they conduct as well are a fertile area for research. Studies normally are undertaken to meet the needs or perceived needs of a manager or decision maker. They may be defined as an organizational intervention normally conducted in response to a request from a manager to know more about an issue relevant to his or her organization or to address the need for action in response to a stimulus of some sort. Studies are initiated for as many reasons as there are managers' personalities, and may be initiated by a single decision maker or by a group consensus.

Formal studies lend themselves to examination more than many organization processes that are begun and concluded behind closed doors and therefore are a rich source of knowledge not only about MA but also about how organizations work. They are significant for a number of reasons. First, studies focus on a problem or opportunity that has been explicitly recognized by one or more decision makers. Second, they require the use of dollar and personnel resources, and often require much time on the part of the decision maker who initiated the effort or is the recipient of the study report. Last, because a written report with findings is usually produced, there is typically documentation of information, methods, and processes, and it is associated with the effort as an organizational intervention.

Our research included choosing one study for in-depth examination from each of the fifteen randomly selected management analysis offices in the federal government.[1] The research was designed to collect and analyze information about the nature and conduct of MA studies in as much detail as possible. Studies were selected on the basis of certain criteria: the purpose of the study had to be to assist in decision making, and it had to be a large study that resulted in a written report with recommendations. In addition, the analyst who conducted the study had to be available for interviews.

The methodology employed in analyzing the fifteen case studies involved structured and unstructured interviews with the head of the MA unit, the analyst who conducted the study, and in most cases the decision maker who received the study (see Appendixes A and B). It also involved obtaining a copy of the study report and examining it along with associated materials (see Appendix C). Each of the studies was examined by means of a similar framework and set of questions. Although tests of statistical significance were not used, the case studies may be considered representative of more-major MA studies designed to assist in decision making in the federal government. The studies are briefly described here, and then their characteristics are discussed and summarized in tabular form.

DESCRIPTION OF THE STUDIES

Study A. A Study of the Timber Presale Process and Procedures Used on the Nez Percé National Forest

This study analyzed the process and procedures used to prepare timberland for sale and cutting. The goal of the study was to make the presale process as efficient and effective as possible so that profit from the sale of timber from the national forest could be maximized. A three-person team conducted the study, which took about one staff year to complete. A detailed report was developed and included narrative, graphs, statistical tables, and flow charts.

Study B. Loan Servicing Study

The purpose of this study was to examine the effectiveness of the policies and procedures used in servicing loans made by the agency under the Public Works and Economic Development Act. The goal of the study was to improve loan servicing. The study was conducted by one management analyst and took four months to complete. A very detailed narrative report was developed with many recommendations.

Study C. Resources Control Center Process Improvement Study

The purpose of the study was to improve the service provided by the Resources Control Center. The center controls and coordinates work requests and purchase requisitions for administrative services. The study was conducted by several management analysts and took nine months to complete. The report included narrative, statistics, dollar amounts, and flow charts.

Study D. A Study of Decentralized Program Evaluation

The study was an effort to improve efficiency, effectiveness, and overall management by analyzing and proposing changes in the areas of centralization and decentralization. Four management analysts conducted the study, which took about one staff year to complete. A detailed report primarily in narrative described the concept of decentralization and recommended changes to the programs.

Study E. Staffing Study of Contracts and Grants Management Branches

The purpose of the study was to assess the staffing levels in two branches and, if necessary, to propose changed staffing levels. The study was conducted by one management analyst and took three staff months to complete. A written report combining narrative and statistical tables and graphs was developed.

Study F. Flexitime Study

The study was an effort to assess the desirability of adopting some form of flexitime on a department-wide basis. Sophisticated methods were used to measure the effect of flexitime on other variables such as the use of leave and quality of service. Approximately twenty-three staff months were spent on the effort. A detailed written report documented the wide range of methods used in conducting the study.

Study G. Reorganization: Review and Planning Study

This was a major study to make improvements in many bureau-wide management systems. Seven study teams were established, consisting of personnel from throughout the bureau. The study teams developed many recommendations that went to the assistant secretary for approval. Two analysts spent over one staff year conducting the study.

Study H. Analysis of Special Agent Investigative Document Paperwork

The study was undertaken to assess the paperwork burden on special agents and reduce it where possible. A team of three analysts conducted the study, which took about one staff year to complete. The report included narrative description combined with statistical tables and dollar costs.

Study I. Report on the Feasibility of Decentralizing Administrative Management Functions

The purpose of this study was to determine the desirability and feasibility of decentralizing functions within administrative management. The study was conducted by one management analyst and required about three staff months. The report documented the research process and recommended a number of changes.

Study J. Task Force on Administrative Personnel

The purpose of the study was to assess policies and procedures about the selection, training, and development of administrative personnel for overseas assignment. A task group was established and chaired by a management analyst. The group developed a report and recommendations for the under secretary for management. Two staff months of analysts' time were required to conduct the study.

Study K. Study of the Rulemaking Process

The study assessed the adequacy of the rulemaking process and made recommendations for improvement. A team of four analysts took about six staff months to complete the study. A detailed narrative report with flow charts was developed.

Study L. An Evaluation of the Detector Dog Program

This broad-based evaluation of the effectiveness of the detector dog program was brought about by problems with high staff turnover. A study team composed of four persons conducted the evaluation. The report contained narrative, statistical tables, and graphs. The study took approximately nine staff months to complete.

Study M. An Economic Analysis of Future Federal Office Space Requirements and Options

The purpose of this study was to develop better ways of estimating federal office space needs and of determining when the lease or building option was preferable. The study was conducted by a four-person interdisciplinary team and took forty-five staff months to complete. The report made recommendations based on statistical analyses.

Study N. A Study of International Affairs Paperwork Flow

A new division chief was intersted in having an analysis of the paperwork flow and functions in order to improve efficiency. The study was conducted by an individual analyst and recommended changes to paperwork procedures and functions. The study required two staff months to complete.

Study O. Survey of the Veterans Benefits Field Examiner Outbasing

The study compared the cost of centralizing the location of field examiners to the current status quo. The study was conducted by one managment analyst and took five staff months to complete. The report combines narrative description with statistical and cost tables.

RESEARCH APPROACH

A review of the literature has revealed few sources dealing with MA studies. Further, an examination of literature of related fields such as program analysis and evaluation uncovered few in-depth examinations of studies or the study process. The following material, then, is of importance for its descriptive value. Although each study is, in a sense, unique, the focus of this research was to examine each study in the light of selected common characteristics, grouped into two areas: kind of study, and methods and processes. Once these attributes are identified, a basis exists for identifying those variables associated with successful and less-successful efforts. The tabular data that provide the basis for the following discussion is in tables 4.1, 4.2, and 4.3.

KINDS OF STUDIES

The kind of study is the first area examined for the fifteen MA efforts. "Kind of study" is defined by five substantive factors: (1) purpose of

Table 4.1
Characteristics of Fifteen Large Management Analysis Studies

STUDIES

	A	B	C	D	E	F	G	H	I	J	K	L	M	N	O	Total Number	Percent
A. Purpose of the Study																	
1. assist in making a specific decision					X					X					X	3	20
2. provide general assistance in defining a problem and making a decision about it	X	X	X	X		X	X	X	X		X	X	X	X		12	80
3. gain acceptance in one part of an organization for a decision made in another part																0	0
																15	
B. Topical Content Area																	
1. work methods and procedures	X	X						X				X		X		5	33
2. systems (automated)																0	0
3. personnel utilization and staffing requirements					X											1	7
4. productivity and performance measurement											X					1	7
5. cost analysis and benefit/cost analysis														X		1	7
6. organization placement, organization structure				X												1	7
7. policy						X			X	X			X			4	27
8. interpersonal relationships and behavioral science																0	0
9. general review or survey																0	0
10. work systems, management systems	X						X									2	14
																15	
C. Initiator of the Study																	
1. top agency or bureau management	X							X				X	X			4	27
2. top administrative management		X	X	X	X							X				5	33
3. top program management											X			X		2	14
4. the unit studied, itself														X		1	7
																15	

Table: categories with study markings (X) across 15 studies, with count and percent columns.

Item	Studies (X = 15)	No.	%
5. the MA unit, itself	X	2	14
6. a combination		0	0
7. top administrative management in a program organization	X	1	7
		15	
D. Organization Location Where Study Was Conducted			
1. a function located organizationally in administrative management	X X X	3	20
2. an administrative function located organizationally under a program area	X	1	7
3. a program function located organizationally under a program area	X X X X X X	6	40
4. bureau or agency-wide	X X X X X	5	33
		15	
E. Organizational Location of the Management Analysis (MA) Unit			
1. under administrative top management	X X X X X X X X X X X X X X	14	93
2. under agency or bureau top management	X	1	7
3. under a program area		0	0
		15	
F. Nature of the Study			
1. prospective analysis, future-oriented	X X X X X X X X X X X X X	13	86
2. retrospective evaluation	X	1	7
3. a combination of 1. and 2.	X	1	7
		15	

the study, (2) topical content area, (3) initiator of the study, (4) organization location where the study was conducted, and (5) retrospective or prospective nature of the study (see Table 4.1).

Purpose of the Study

The first question addressed was that of the general purpose of the study. Most of the studies provided assistance in defining and conceptualizing the problem as well as on making a decision about it. This suggests the problems were of a complex nature and that the initiator of the study had not already developed a clear definition of the problem. None of the management analysts who conducted the studies felt that the purpose of the study was to gain acceptance for a decision that had already been made in another part of the organization.

Study Topics

Although MA is often associated with methods and procedures efforts, studies can cover a wide range of topics. The most frequently occurring topics were the five studies that dealt with work methods and procedures and the four studies dealing with policy. Two studies dealt with work/management systems, while one study each fell in the topical areas of productivity and performance measurement, cost analysis, organization placement, and personal staffing.

Initiator of the Study

Five of the fifteen studies were initiated by top administrative management. Top agency or bureau management was the next most frequent initiator of studies, with four of the fifteen. Clearly, top management initiates most major management analysis efforts for decision-making purposes.

Where Studies Were Conducted

The fourth question concerned location of the organization where the study was conducted. Six of the fifteen studies were of program functions located organizationally in program areas. Five of the studies were of bureau or agency-wide questions. Of the remaining studies, three were conducted in administrative management areas and one was of an administrative function located in a program area. Although MA is frequently associated with administrative management, most of these studies were of bureau- and/or agency-wide issues.

Prospective or Retrospective Direction

The last question dealt with the prospective or retrospective nature of the study. Prospective analysis focus on proposing changes to the status quo as opposed to retrospective evaluation. Thirteen studies were prospective or future-oriented. MA is essentially a prospective activity.

STUDY METHODS

The methods used in MA studies is the next area examined. For the purposes of this research, methods are defined as the activities carried out in the course of the study. More than one method was used in all of the studies, and the use of one method, therefore, does not exclude the use of others (see Table 4.2).

The scientific method formed the basis for examining the MA studies. The scientific method, simply stated, is composed of the following steps or procedures carried out in all studies: definition of the problem, collection of information about the problem, analysis of information collected, and development of conclusions and recommendations. The examination is divided into two parts: the methods used and the process defined in terms of who was involved in making decisions about the study and who actually conducted its various phases (see Appendix B).

How the Problem Was Structured

The two most common ways to structure management problems were to describe them in narrative and to use a descriptive model, such as a flow chart or diagram. Thirteen of the studies used flow charts or other descriptive models. The methodology in five of the fifteen studies involved exploring numerical relationships among variables as a way of structuring the study. One study out of the fifteen developed a predictive model using a regression model.

Methods of Information Collection

Information collection, of course, is a fundamental part of any problem-solving effort. The most common method of information collection was interviews. Thirteen of the fifteen studies used structured interviews. Other commonly used methods for information collection were examining manuals and program documentation and examining existing narrative and statistical records. Questionnaires were used in only three of the fifteen studies. Statistical sampling was used in four studies, and the gathering of empirical statistical data was used in two

Table 4.2
Methods Used in Fifteen Large Management Analysis Studies

S T U D I E S

	A	B	C	D	E	F	G	H	I	J	K	L	M	N	O	Total Number	Percent
A. How was the problem structured?																	
1. not structured		X			X		X		X							4	33
2. described in narrative	X	X	X	X	X	X	X	X	X	X	X	X		X	X	13	87
3. descriptive model	X		X	X		X					X	X				6	40
4. quantitative relationships among variables	X											X	X	X	X	5	33
5. predictive model													X			1	7
B. What methods were used in information collection?																	
1. manuals, written documentation	X	X	X		X	X	X	X	X	X		X		X	X	11	73
2. literature review						X	X		X			X	X			5	33
3. examine existing narrative records	X		X	X	X	X				X		X	X	X	X	10	67
4. examine existing statistical records	X		X	X	X	X		X		X		X	X	X	X	11	73
5. participant observation			X													1	7
6. brainstorming sessions							X									1	7
7. unstructured interviews		X			X		X		X	X		X				6	40
8. structured interviews	X	X	X		X	X	X	X	X	X		X		X	X	13	87
9. unstructured questionnaires						X											
10. structured questionnaires													X	X	X	3	20
11. statistical sampling			X					X					X		X	4	27
12. gathering of empirical statistical data			X			X										2	13
13. set up experiment						X										1	7

50

S T U D I E S

	A	B	C	D	E	F	G	H	I	J	K	L	M	N	O	Total Number	Percent
C. What kind of information was collected?																	
1. ideas in brainstorming sessions							X									1	7
2. qualitative comments in interviews	X	X	X		X	X	X		X	X	X	X		X	X	12	80
3. narrative comments on questionnaires					X				X							2	13
4. qualitative data from secondary sources	X	X	X		X	X	X		X		X	X		X	X	11	73
5. quantitative data from secondary sources	X		X	X	X	X		X		X	X	X	X	X	X	12	80
6. empirically gathered statistics						X									X	3	20
7. dollar costs	X							X				X	X		X	5	33
8. dollar costs - dollar benefits																0	0
9. experimental						X						X				1	7
D. How was the information ordered, analyzed?																	
1. the information was not summarized; raw data were used		X					X		X	X						4	27
2. information was summarized in narrative	X	X	X	X	X	X	X	X	X	X	X	X	X	X	X	15	100
3. statistics	X	X	X		X	X		X	X		X	X	X	X	X	9	60
4. costs and benefits were described in narrative												X	X		X	3	20
5. costs were quantified	X							X				X			X	4	27
6. cost and benefits were quantified in dollars																0	

51

Table 4.2 (continued)

		A	B	C	D	E	F	G	H	I	J	K	L	M	N	O	Total Number	Percent
E.	**What methods were used in ordering, analyzing, and interpreting statistical data?**																	
1.	none; raw data were used		X					X		X	X		X		X		6	40
2.	the intuition and judgment		X	X	X	X	X	X		X	X	X	X		X		11	73
3.	descriptive statistics	X		X	X	X	X		X	X	X		X		X		9	60
4.	inferential statistics			X			X										2	13
5.	cost analysis	X							X				X			X	4	27
6.	present-value analysis													X			1	7
7.	correlation													X	X		2	13
8.	regression													X			1	7
F.	**What was the basis for the conclusions and recommendations?**																	
1.	the judgment of the analyst/team members		X	X	X	X	X	X		X	X	X	X		X		11	73
2.	consultation between the analyst and unit chief or personnel in the unit studied	X	X			X							X		X		5	33
3.	consultation with the decision makers							X		X		X					3	20
4.	were obvious from the narrative information					X			X	X		X					4	27
5.	were obvious from numerical data	X					X		X				X	X	X	X	7	47
6.	a statistical analysis of the data			X									X	X			3	20

STUDIES

Figure 4.1
Use of Multiple Methods for Information Collection

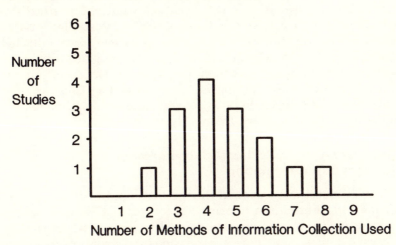

Number of Methods of Information Collection Used

studies. One study used an experimental method that compared treated and untreated groups. On the average narrative, qualitative information, such as that gathered from interviews and manuals and program documentation, was used more than statistical and numerical information.

There was considerable variation in the number of methods used in the different studies. The number of methods ranged from two to eight. Five studies used four methods to collect information, while four studies used fewer and six studies used more. A frequency distribution of the number of methods used to collect information is in Figure 4.1.

Kind of Information Collected

The next question dealt with was the kind of information collected. This question is related to the methods used in information collection; particular study methods are more appropriate than others for gathering certain kinds of information. For example, interviews are normally used to gather qualitative narrative information, while an experiment is usually used to collect quantitative information. The range of elements in this category runs from "ideas in brainstorming sessions" to experimental information. Qualitative comments from interviews were the most common kind of information collected in the studies. Twelve studies collected qualitative comments in interviews. The second most common kind of information collected was quantitative data from secondary sources such as accounting records. Qualitative data from secondary sources was the third most frequently employed, being used in seven of the fifteen studies. Empirically gathered statistics were collected in three of the fifteen studies. Five of the studies collected dollar cost information. Only one study collected experimental data. Overall, the use of descriptive, qualitative information was more common, although a significant portion of the studies collected quantitative information from secondary sources. For example, five studies used dollar costs and occasionally benefits. Experimental data were not used frequently.

Approaches to Ordering, Analyzing, and Interpreting Information

The next question concerned the methods used in ordering, analyzing, and interpreting the information collected. Although methods of analyzing and interpreting data depend in part on the nature of the data, various methods of data analysis and interpretation are available.

Several ways of ordering and analyzing data were arrayed, ranging from using raw data to the use of regression analysis. The two most frequently used approaches analyzing and interpreting data were the intuition and judgment of the analyst and descriptive statistics. They were used in eleven and nine of the studies respectively. Inferential statistics were used in two of the fifteen studies, while some form of cost or benefit/cost analysis was used in three studies. Regression analysis and present value analysis were used in just one of the studies. The more nonscientific methods, such as the intuition and judgment of the analyst and descriptive statistics, were used more than quantitative tools from statistics and economics, such as inferential statistics, benefit/cost analysis, and present value analysis.

The Basis for Conclusions and Recommendations

The final question dealt with the basis for the study findings. The most frequently cited basis for conclusions was the judgment of the analyst/team members, used in eleven of the fifteen studies. The second most frequently cited answer was "findings were obvious from the numerical data," which was cited in eight of the studies. In four of the studies analysts believed the conclusions and recommendations were obvious from the descriptive information.

INTERPERSONAL PROCESSES

Next, the interpersonal processes used in conducting the study were analyzed. The term *process* refers to who was involved in making decisions about planning and conducting the study and also refers to who carried out important phases of the study as well as the way it was done. Process questions follow the traditional steps in conducting a study, beginning with "Who defined the problem?" Studies frequently used more than one process, and the use of one process does not mean others are excluded (see Table 4.3).

Who Defined the Problem?

In nine of the fifteen studies, individual analysts or teams of analysts were responsible for defining the problem. In five cases the problem definition was the responsibility of an inter-unit team or jointly of the analyst and the person requesting the study or the analyst and personnel in the unit being studied. In one case the person requesting the study was considered responsible for problem definition.

Problem Definition Process

The next question posed was "By what process was the problem defined?" The processes were arrayed and ranged from "by the analyst individually" to "meetings between the analyst and the personnel in the unit being studied." The "analyst individually" defined the problem in three of the studies. In ten studies the problem was defined by meetings between the analyst and the chief of the unit being studied or the decision maker. Meetings between the analyst and personnel in the unit studied and an interunit study team were part of the problem definition process in one study each.

Who Collected the Information?

An important aspect of the quality and credibility of any study is that of who collected the information. Individual analysts or teams of analysts were solely responsible for collecting information in eight of fifteen studies, over half the total. Members of an inter-unit study team were solely responsible for information collection in two additional studies. These data suggest that the task of information collection is ordinarily done by the professional analysts and is not, for example, delegated to the unit studied. Also, analysts were responsible for deciding what information would be collected in three-quarters of the cases.

Analysis and Interpretation of the Data

Data interpretation and analysis is one of the most critical aspects of conducting a study. The perspective and affiliation of the individuals

Table 4.3
Processes Used in Fifteen Large Management Analysis Studies

	STUDIES															Total Number	Percent
	A	B	C	D	E	F	G	H	I	J	K	L	M	N	O		
A. Who defined the problem?																	
1. person requesting the study									X						X	2	13
2. management analyst			X	X	X	X		X	X	X			X	X		9	60
3. team of analysts	X			X		X										3	20
4. inter-unit study team							X									1	7
5. both the management analyst and the person requesting the study	X											X				2	13
6. the management analyst and personnel in the unit being studied		X			X											2	13
B. By what process was the problem defined?																	
1. by the decision maker alone																0	0
2. by the analyst individually		X	X	X	X	X		X		X						7	47
3. by inter-unit study team meetings							X			X						2	13
4. by meetings between the analyst and chief of unit studied	X				X	X			X	X	X					6	40
5. by meeting between analyst and decision maker					X	X		X	X			X	X			5	33
6. by meeting between analyst and personnel in the unit being studied		X														1	7
C. Who collected the information (data)?																	
1. the analyst		X			X		X								X	4	27
2. team of analysts	X	X	X	X		X		X		X		X				7	47
3. members of inter-unit study team						X					X	X				3	20
4. the analyst and the head of the unit being studied					X	X				X						3	20
5. a joint effort by the analyst and several personnel in the unit being studied												X		X		2	13

D. How was it decided what information would be collected?

	A	B	C	D	E	F	G	H	I	J	K	L	M	N	O	Number	Percent
1. by the analyst individually	X	X			X				X	X	X			X	X	8	53
2. by a team of analysts			X	X		X	X						X			5	33
3. by an inter-unit study team							X	X				X				3	20
4. by the analyst in consultation with the chief of the unit being studied												X				1	7
5. by the analyst in consultation with personnel in the unit being studied																0	0

E. Who ordered, analyzed, and interpreted the data?

	A	B	C	D	E	F	G	H	I	J	K	L	M	N	O	Number	Percent
1. the analyst		X	X	X	X	X	X	X	X							8	53
2. a team of analysts	X									X	X	X	X		X	6	40
3. an inter-unit study team							X		X			X				3	20
4. the analyst and the chief in the unit being studied								X								1	7
5. the analyst and the decision maker																0	0
6. a group composed of the analyst and personnel in the unit being studied														X		1	7

F. How was it decided how the data would be ordered, analyzed and interpreted?

	A	B	C	D	E	F	G	H	I	J	K	L	M	N	O	Number	Percent
1. by the analyst alone	X	X			X			X	X	X	X			X	X	9	60
2. by a team of analysts in meetings			X	X		X						X	X			5	33
3. by an inter-unit study team in meetings							X					X				2	13
4. by the analyst in consultation with the chief of the unit being studied																0	0
5. by the analyst in consultation with personnel in the unit studied																0	0

57

Table 4.3 (continued)

	STUDIES															Total Number	Percent
	A	B	C	D	E	F	G	H	I	J	K	L	M	N	O		
G. Who developed the conclusions and recommendations?																	
1. the analyst	X				X	X	X	X	X	X					X	8	53
2. a team of analysts	X		X	X	X	X							X			6	40
3. the analyst and the decision maker							X				X				X	3	20
4. an inter-unit study team									X	X		X				3	20
5. the analyst and the chief of the unit studied					X				X							2	13
6. the analyst and personnel in the unit being studied														X		1	7
H. By what process were the conclusions and recommendations developed?																	
1. the analyst alone	X				X			X	X			X	X	X		7	47
2. a team of analysts together			X	X							X					3	20
3. an inter-unit study team						X				X		X				3	20
4. analysts/study team in consultation with the decision maker					X	X			X							3	20
5. the analyst in consultation with the chief of the unit being studied	X				X			X				X			X	5	33
6. the analyst meeting with personnel in the unit being studied														X		1	7

who perform this function can greatly influence study design. The question posed was "Who ordered, analyzed, and interpreted the data?" The analyst or team of analysts were solely responsible for analyzing and interpreting the data in ten of the fifteen studies. In three studies the inter-unit study teams were responsible for the analysis. In only one study was the chief or personnel from the unit studied responsible for data analysis. In all of the studies the analyst took the lead in carrying out data analysis.

Decisions about How the Data Would Be Analyzed and Interpreted

The decision about how data will be analyzed and interpreted is one of the most important in studies. The actors involved in this phase of the study can have much influence on the study findings. The question posed was, "Who decided how the data would be ordered, analyzed and interpreted?" In thirteen of fifteen cases, the decision was made by analysts or teams of analysts. In two cases the decision was made by an inter-unit study team. In no case was the decision about data analysis made in consultation with the chief of the unit studied or in consultation with personnel in the unit studied except if they were on an interunit study team. Thus the decision about how data would be analyzed was made by management analysts in almost all cases.

Who Developed the Conclusions and Recommendations?

The last phase in most studies has to do with the development of conclusions and recommendations. All of the studies reviewed had recommendations in addition to conclusions, which suggests they were action documents. Each recommendation proposed change to the status quo.

In eight of the fifteen studies individual analysts or teams of analysts were responsible for developing the recommendations. In all other studies the decision maker, chief of the unit studied, or personnel from the unit studied together with the analyst were responsible for developing the recommendations. Thus, clients and decision makers as well as the analyst were responsible for developing conclusions and recommendations in about half the cases.

The Process by Which Conclusions and Recommendations Were Developed

The process by which conclusions and recommendations are developed is certainly one of the most critical in the study process. An effective, meaningful process can make a study useful, while an ineffective process can make a good study useless. In six of the fifteen studies an analyst or a team of analysts working alone developed the conclusions and recommendations. In eight of the studies the analyst developed conclusions and recommendations in consultation with the chief of the unit studied or with the decision maker. In one study an inter-unit study team developed conclusions and recommendations. Thus, while the analyst provided the focus in the development of conclusions and recommendations, in about half the cases the chief or personnel from the unit studied or the decision maker was involved in the process.

CONCLUSIONS ABOUT MANAGEMENT ANALYSTS STUDIES

The topics studied and the methods and processes used suggest the approaches used by analysts in assisting managers to solve organizational problems and to seize opportunities. Conclusions pertaining to the general nature of these studies are:

1. Most studies provided general assistance in defining a problem and making a decision about it rather than focusing on a very specific decision.
2. Work methods and procedures studies were the single most numerous type of study.
3. The majority of the studies were initiated by top administrative management or by bureau top management.
4. Most of studies were carried out in program areas or concerned bureauwide issues. A minority of the studies were connected with administrative management issues.
5. The preponderance of studies were prospective, or future oriented, as opposed to retrospective evaluations.

Conclusions regarding the methods and processes are:

1. Most of the MA studies took a descriptive approach in addressing management problems.
2. The most common method of information collection was structured interviews. Other commonly used methods were the examination of manuals, written documentation, and existing narrative and statistical records.
3. Questionnaires, statistical sampling, benefit/cost analysis and experimental designs were used less frequently.
4. Although management analysts were responsible for defining the problem to be studied in the preponderance of cases, the process involved working with the client or the decision maker.

5. The collection of information was handled solely by analysts in most cases.
6. Decisions about data collection and analysis were usually made solely by analysts.
7. Although analysts were responsible for developing conclusions and recommendations, the process frequently involved consulting with the client or decision maker.
8. The client or decision maker appears to be involved in the beginning and closing phases of management studies (problem definition and development of conclusions and recommendations), while data collection and analysis and interpretation phases are handled solely by the analysts.

The analysis of MA studies also provides a number of broader conclusions. First, MA is sometimes perceived as almost exclusively associated with administrative questions. The studies examined in this research suggest that management analyses are often of important program, policy, and management issues and that MA often has influence outside the administrative arena. MA units appear to provide important analytical services associated with the agency mission.

A second conclusion pertains to the size of studies conducted. The scope, depth, and staff time devoted to studies were greater than the researcher anticipated. Several of the studies required more than one staff year of analysts' time. Further, several of the studies involved inter-unit study teams and had the deep involvement of top management. Considering the time of analysts, decision makers, personnel who provided information for the studies, and administrative and clerical support personnel, the total effort devoted to these studies was very substantial.

Overall, the methods used in the studies were in accord with the researcher's expectations. The studies made extensive use of interviews and existing narrative and statistical reports with little use of quantitative experimental designs. The methods of data analysis were straightforward and suitable for communicating with managers. The study methods used, in general, reflect the purpose of management analysis: to help decision makers solve management problems.

NOTE

1. Oman, Ray C., "The Nature, Conduct, and Acceptance of Management Analysis Studies in Civilian Federal Agencies," unpublished doctoral dissertation, The George Washington University, Washington, D.C., 1983.

CHAPTER 5 _____

Automation: A Familiar
Technology Grows in Importance

Computers have become commonplace over the past decade, owing in part to high-power advertising and mass media coverage. It is easy to forget that computers are not new but have been in use for several decades, although their focus has changed over the years. Perhaps the first example of the use of a computer for large-scale data processing was the Holerith machine, which processed data collected in the census of 1890. The birth of the electronic digital computer, of course, followed that of mechanical devices for data processing, but it too has been with us for some time. An article in the *Washington Post*, "Honoring the Father of the Computer, 50 Years Late," gave credit to John V. Atanasoff for his work inventing computers at Iowa State University in 1937.[1] Further work by others, such as John Mauchly, resulted in the first digital computer, the Electronic Numerical Integrator and Computer (ENIAC) used by the U.S. Army in 1946. Although many computer buzzwords have come and gone, the term *automation* is generic and covers the evolution of computers from the first Holerith machine to the latest microcomputer or personal computer (PC). Despite the trends and fads that have characterized the various phases automation has passed through, there are certain commonalities that apply wherever it is used.

Automation in particular is not new to management analysts, who have been centrally involved with automation since it began to spread throughout the federal government just after World War II. In fact, the methods examiners and efficiency experts, who were predecessors of today's management analysts, almost certainly were involved with the use of the Holerith machine to process census data. Automation has, of course, led to the development of totally new job fields, such as those of computer programmer, computer specialist, and systems analyst. Aside from these new fields that are entirely related to computers, management analysis (MA) is probably more closely associated with automation than is any other professional field. Very recently other new fields, such as information systems analysis, designed to meet emerging needs and encompassing a broader view of automation closer to that of management analysis, have begun to emerge in the federal government.

Automation began to grow rapidly at about the same time that MA developed as a distinct field in the federal government. In some ways the emergence and development of MA and of automation parallel each other. The strongest link is that automation affects the way work is done, and MA is concerned with work processes in organizations. A study of MA done in 1959 showed that efforts involving computers were the second largest category of work done by management analysts.[2] Similarly, if a survey of MA were done today, one of the most important areas covered would be automation and computers.

The focus of automation in the federal government has changed considerably over the years, partly as a result of the evolution of the technology. For example, the early applications of automation involved such tasks as the processing of census data and the computerization of payroll and accounting reports. In the early days, two criteria were commonly used to select candidates for automation: the processing of vast amounts of data that could be done more quickly and accurately on computer than by hand, and the performance of repetitive tasks when the parameters remained the same. As the use of computers spread throughout the federal government, their tasks and functions broadened and became more varied and often less tangible. For example, computer applications spread from printing paychecks to developing automated information systems and management information systems (MIS). MIS was a computer buzzword for many years. More recently, of course, hot applications for computers have included project management systems, expert systems, and artificial intelligence.

THE ROLE OF MANAGEMENT ANALYSIS
IN AUTOMATION

Previously in this chapter we talked mainly about computer applications, not computer hardware, software, or the interoperability of systems. The aspect of computers that MA is primarily concerned with is the capability of the technology to perform a task or function in a better way. The primary link between the work of a management analyst and automation is the use of computers to perform work better to meet organization objectives. This central link between MA and computers existed in the early days of their development and is still present today.

The role of the management analyst in relation to automation is most often that of the "intelligent generalist" or that of the "middle man" between management or users of the automated system and the specialists who run it. Although computers have led to the development of new fields, MA can stand alone as a field and is not wedded to any particular technology. In fact, the good analyst identifies a variety of alternative solutions to problems and then assists management in making a decision based on one or more criteria, which are usually associated with cost-effectiveness. In solving a generic problem or seizing an opportunity, computer technology may be one alternative solution the analyst considers among others that might include, for example, a better manual technology, a change of work process or procedures, a better recruitment program, or more training for personnel.

The two most basic understandings the analyst must have about automation are how it can improve the job performance of the analyst himself and how it can improve bottom-line effectiveness and efficiency in any part of the organization. The first may be seen as a micro perspective, while the second can be viewed a macro point of view.

Yet, there is obviously overlap and crossover between these two fundamental perspectives. For example, there is a relationship between the analyst's ability to use automation to improve his or her own productivity and the ability to see how automation can enhance the jobs, tasks, or functions of others. Further, the knowledge of how intelligently to apply automation on a small scale can assist in applying it on a large or organization-wide scale. Insight into the benefits and shortcomings of automation gained at one's own work station can be fruitfully applied to questions of division- or department-wide automation. Conversely, a synergism also exists between one's knowledge of the use of automation elsewhere in the organization and development of useful applications at one's own work station.

The analyst's involvement with automation on a microlevel will be treated first. A discussion of how automation can be used to improve overall organization performance will follow.

The analyst should have a plan for how the automated equipment is to be used before it is ordered. For example, the analyst will have a list of applications lending themselves to automation. If it is word processing (WP), the first application may be for writing study reports. If it is a statistical package, the analyst will have thought of several studies in which the computation of statistics, such as standard deviation, present value analysis, or coefficient of correlation, would prove useful. Or, if it is a data base package, the analyst will have thought through the kinds of data that could be maintained on the system and how it would meet a real management need.

The analyst should be trained in the automated system that will be used. If a WP system is being installed the analyst should brush up on typing skills as well as have training in the particular WP package. If the automation is a statistical package the analyst should be trained in the appropriate statistical technique(s) whether it be present value analysis or correlation and regression. A humorous example of a computer program going beyond the knowledge of its users comes to mind. This author observed a group of three senior professionals gathered around a PC anxiously waiting for the computation of a coefficient of correlation. The computation took several minutes, during which time the three professionals exchanged ideas, bantered, and anxiously speculated on what the result would be. When the answer came out, it was +.1. During the discussion that followed, it became evident that none of the three had the slightest idea what a statistical coefficient of correlation meant, that it can range between +1.0 and −1.0, what the sign, + or −, indicates, and that a coefficient of .1 is so low it generally cannot be used for statistical inference. Obviously, an automated statistical program can not be effective unless the users know enough about the statistics behind it to interpret the results.

To be effective in the area of automation on the macrolevel, the analyst must apply some of the same analytical skills that are critical to other parts of his job. Automation and computers may be seen as a special-case application of the analytical tools of the management analyst. The principles involving the use of the scientific method to analyze and solve problems that were discussed in the chapters on studies apply here. Because management analysts are concerned with using automation as a tool to improve organization performance, they find themselves more involved with some aspects of automation than others. The items listed below are suggestive of some of the areas with which analysts are most frequently concerned:

1. defining the needs and requirements of users for automated systems;

2. planning organization initiatives in automation and information systems;

3. analyzing the costs and benefits of proposed systems;

4. evaluating alternative systems to determine the most cost-effective one once a decision is made to automate;

5. analyzing of information stored in an automated data base or MIS;

6. measuring the effectiveness and efficiency and value to the organization of existing systems;

7. developing approaches to use life-cycle management principles with automated systems; and

8. working in the broader area of information resource management (IRM).

As suggested by the above list, management analysts are centrally involved with issues concerning the need for the system, the choice of the best system, having the system meet user needs, and the analysis and evaluation of the system during its life cycle. Four of these topics are elaborated on in the following paragraphs.

DEFINING AND MEASURING USER NEEDS

Probably the first and most basic aspect of automation with which management analysts are concerned is that of defining and measuring the need for new systems. Automation, of course, has been a flashy item during most of its history, and many organizations have chosen to jump on the bandwagon without any careful analysis of benefits or costs. The usual scenario for acquiring a system has included a proponent, frequently the computer services organization element, who advocated the new system. If the proponent was articulate and powerful, any study of the need for a new system was simply a justification rather than an objective analysis. In the federal government much of the analysis, however sketchy, was done by management analysts. Recently, however, organizations have been taking a harder look at the need for automated systems because of tight budgets and a growing awareness of the high cost of such systems, many of which are hidden or are not evident until well into the system life cycle.[3]

With the growing interest in assessing the need for automation and information systems, the role of the objective analyst has been legitimized as the demand for good studies has increased.[4] Since most automation efforts in the government service-producing organizations are concerned with information rather than automating an industrial process, the focus of this discussion is on information systems. Information has always been central to MA with its concern for management studies and decision making. So, it comes natural to most analysts to assess the information needs of managers and workers at all levels. Analysts are experienced in data-gathering techniques such as interviewing and administering questionnaires, the very techniques used to assess demand for information.

In assessing information needs, analysts face the dilemma of how to place a value on the information desired. Here, the analyst in the real world is required to apply the two old rules of thumb about when to use automation: "Is the information needed repetitively or is it a one-time request?" and "Is the volume of information required such that

Figure 5.1
Cost and Value of Information

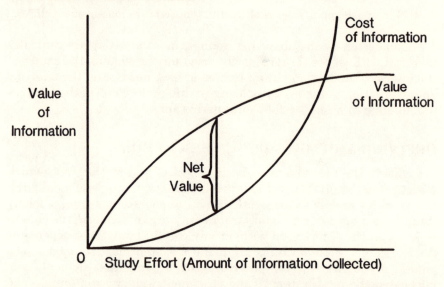

it can best be handled and processed by automated means?" The rubber meets the road here; the analyst must be both creative and critical in assessing the value of the information in view of the cost of acquiring it. Naturally, the experienced analyst can apply the notion of decreasing marginal value for each additional increment of information (see Figure 5.1). No matter how important the information provided, at some point its value is less than the cost of getting it. Since the value of information to the organization is at best difficult to quantify, the analyst normally must be satisfied with surrogate measures, such as the number of personnel needing the information, the level in the organization where the need exists, the frequency and importance of the need, and the nature of the information itself. On the other hand, even gross measurement can often give a good indication of the value of the information to the organization. For example, information clearly has considerable potential value if it is needed routinely by many top management personnel for making basic decisions about the ongoing program. On the other hand, information that is needed only by two or three personnel once or twice a year has relatively little value.

AUTOMATION PLANNING

Automation planning often requires more technical knowledge than general organization or strategic planning and, therefore, is often best handled as an interdisciplinary effort. Again, the analyst's grasp of the "need" for information or for an automated system is the basis on which effective planning is carried out. The "user needs assessment" referred to above is often conducted by management analysts and leads naturally into planning alternative ways to meet the defined need. The management analyst's traditional involvement with defining objectives, such as management by objectives (MBO) and other such efforts, is another key element in the planning process. When needs and objectives are properly defined, a planning effort is well on its way to success.

Technology assessment, one of the more technical aspects of automation planning for estimating the future trends and directions in automation, should be an interdisciplinary effort. Computer specialists or experts in areas such as computer hardware, software, and telecommunications need to be involved in this area of automation planning. In these more-technical areas, the role of the management analyst can include providing input on how future technology can best be applied given the mission, objectives, activities, and personnel of the particular organization. Automation planning is just one element of a good overall planning process, which includes strategic planning and which may have intermediate and short-range objectives as well as detailed action plans. The analyst is ideally equipped for the job of integrating automation planning into the overall organization planning efforts. The effect of technology and automation on individual jobs, the work process and procedures, and, ultimately, of organization structure are fertile areas for research in MA.

ANALYZING THE BENEFITS AND COSTS OF PROPOSED SYSTEMS

For many years in the federal government there was little rigorous, objective analyst of the benefits and costs of proposed automated systems. Most bureaucrats fell into one of two categories. First, there were those who felt that their organizations should acquire automated systems for the same reasons that they, themselves, had televisions in their homes and two cars in their garages. The underlying idea was that it was part of the American way to acquire new technology, it was part of our culture, and, after all, we had to keep up with the Joneses. The second group of bureaucrats was composed of those who thought that new technology resulted in greatly increased productivity and thus was necessarily cost-effective. The underlying premise here was that technology had greatly increased the productivity of U.S. agriculture and manufacturing and, therefore, automation as a new technology would have a similar effect in our offices and service producing organizations.

It has taken much time, numerous studies of the effect of automation on white-collar productivity, tight budgets, and a growing awareness of the high cost of computers for bureaucrats to begin to question their assumptions about the value of new technology.[5] Many analysts and most economists have had doubts for some time about the value to organizations of large, unplanned, and inadequately evaluated investments in computers and automation. Finally, tight budgets, increased cost-consciousness, and the results of many studies (which showed no increase or only very marginal increases in productivity due to automation) have begun to attract management's attention. Thus, the time is ripe for analysts to have an impact by helping to implement a more rational approach to investment decisions involving automation.

One reason it took so long for many managers and decision makers to question expenses for automation was that accounting systems seldom revealed the real cost. Costs were often reported in a piecemeal fashion, cost estimates were far less than actual costs, and training and learning-curve costs were seldom considered. Recently, however, articles have begun to appear about the true total cost of investments in various kinds of automation. More and more organizations are realizing that a substantial part of their budgets is going for automation and computers, and managers are beginning to ask if they are getting their money's worth.

There is no reason, of course, why automation cannot be well employed to help organizations meet their goals. The fact that many investments in automation have not been cost-effective is in large part a reflection on management. Well-managed organizations tend to make good use of automation, while many poorly managed ones make bad investments in automation because they expect it to solve deep-seated problems. For years good analysts have been telling managers to view automation as a tool that should compete with other investment alternatives in its ability to meet needs. We all can think of cases where automation judiciously applied produced a good return. The problem is that automation has been too often applied in wholesale fashion with little real thought or planning about how it would be used or how to integrate it into the work processes.

It was suggested in the Introduction that management in many U.S. organizations needed to improve, especially in relation to that of foreign firms. Computers and automation have been long on aggressive advertising and short on objective, rigorous analysis. Automation is a classic example of how a potentially useful tool has in many cases failed to be used in an efficient or cost-effective way.

The decision to invest in automation should generally be handled on a case-by-case basis. Each organization is in some ways unique and is composed of its own mix of mission and goals, policy, procedures, technology, and personnel. There are, however, a few basic concepts, models, and suggestions that are general enough to be applied in most situations.

First, a comprehensive analysis should be done of the costs of any proposed system. This includes listing and trying to quantify as many costs of the proposed system as possible and working closely with potential suppliers who will be inclined to underestimate costs. Quantifiable costs will include obvious items such as equipment and peripherals, software, system maintenance and operation, supplies, and space and utility costs, as well as less obvious and harder to quantify costs such as those associated with training, the learning curve for employees who use the new technology, the additional burden of having to administer and manage a new system, and the dislocations and inconveniences that always result from having to change from one system to another. All costs that can be quantified should be, while those costs not able to be quantified can be listed as qualitative disadvantages or costs. After a total cost of the system is computed, these qualitative costs can be considered subjectively in the decision. Since acquiring, installing, and making a new system operational is not an easy or predictable activity, it is sometimes wise to add a percentage, say 10 or 15 percent, to the computed total cost to get a more accurate estimate. In reality, almost all cost estimates for new or altered systems fall short of the actual cost, so it is prudent to add in an additional cost to cover the error factor. Of course, if the costs occur over a number of years and at different points in time than the benefits, present-value analysis will be helpful in drawing comparisons between systems.

All of the positive aspects or expected benefits of the proposed system should be listed and as many of the benefits quantified as possible. In any objective study, as much effort should go into identifying benefits as was devoted to the cost analysis. It is usually more difficult to quantify benefits than costs, but every effort should be made to identify and quantify them. Benefits of a new system might include being able to do a job faster, being able to do something that was not done before (for example, computing the present value of benefit and cost streams), being able to do a job better, and saving user's time by having more accessible information or easier to read reports. The list of expected benefits should not be pie in the sky. If benefits cannot be made explicit before the system is acquired, they seldom become evident afterward. In a sense, the benefits are the goals for the system, and if the goals cannot be identified, the organization has no way of knowing what it expects from the system and, consequently, will get little out of it. In

Figure 5.2
Benefits Remain the Same and Costs Decrease

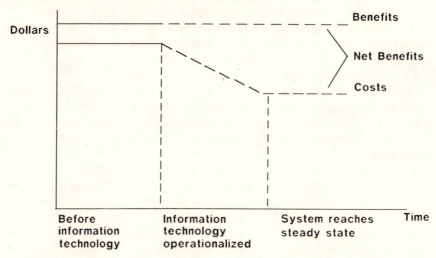

other words, many of the general principles of good management apply equally well to managing the selection and acquisition of a new system. This discussion of benefits and costs obviously does not attempt to cover procurement or acquisition issues arising from dealings with vendors.

The benefits and costs of the proposed system then have to be compared on the basis of decision-making criteria such as net benefits, benefit/cost ratio, or internal rate of return. It is most meaningful, of course, to compare the benefits and costs over the life cycle of the system. However, even if it is difficult to estimate the system life cycle, it is still helpful to compare the benefits and costs on an annual or average annual basis without using the complete life cycle of the system.

Three basic models portrayed graphically can be used to depict the relationship between benefits and costs. Each model is based on a set of assumptions that users, analysts, or decision makers have about proposed automated systems. The first and most basic model assumes that the proposed system will provide the same quantity and quality of product or service as the existing system, but that it will do it at reduced cost. The classic example of this model occurs when the vendor claims his or her system can do just as good a job as the current one but at less cost. If the claim turns out to be true, the organization should see a reduction in out-of-pocket costs with the same level of production and service (see Figure 5.2).

The second model assumes that costs will remain the same but that the proposed system will improve the quantity and quality of product

Figure 5.3
Benefits Increase and Costs Remain the Same

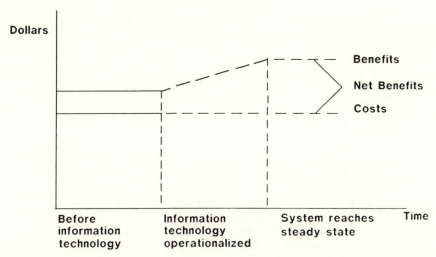

or service provided. In this case the vendor claims his or her system can do a better job at the same cost of the current system. If the claim is correct, the organization should experience improved production and service with no increase in cost (see Figure 5.3).

The third model is the most realistic and assumes that costs will increase with the new system, but that value of the improved quantity and quality of the product or service provided will be greater than the increase in cost. This model is more realistic because proposals for new or modified systems almost always have a higher price tag. Because the analyst or decision maker knows the cost will go up, often significantly, it is critical to identify the substantial benefits that should result. In theory there would be no basis for acquiring the proposed system unless the value of the improved product or service was greater than the increased cost (see Figure 5.4).

INFORMATION RESOURCE MANAGEMENT: A HIGH-GROWTH AREA

Much of what happens with computers and automation in public and private organizations today occurs under the rubric of information resource management (IRM). IRM forms the conceptual and, often, the organizational umbrella under which most ADP initiatives are planned and implemented. While IRM organizational units have been spreading throughout most government agencies and many private firms over the past decade, IRM and information management programs have

Figure 5.4
Both Benefits and Costs Increase

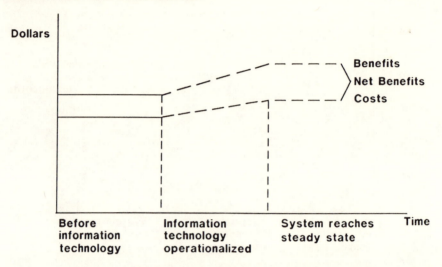

been started at colleges and universities around the country. Thus, IRM is legitimized to the degree that there are programs devoted to teaching it in academic environments, while operational organizations are practicing it in the real world. A considerable number of management analysts currently work in IRM organizations, while others work on information management initiatives although residing in other organization units. In the future there will be expanding opportunities for analysts as the area matures and as pressures from the environment demand better management and analytical techniques to meet organizational needs.

IRM first emerged in the mid- and late 1970s. During that period it became apparent that extensive data collection by the federal government from firms and individuals was imposing a considerable burden on the private sector. Aside from the surveys by data collection agencies such as the Bureau of the Census, other government agencies also frequently requested various kinds of information from the public. It was also apparent that the government itself was spending considerable resources collecting and processing all this information. The birth of IRM was also prompted by reports and regulations governing the treatment of information in the federal government such as the Report of the Commission on Federal Paperwork, the Privacy Act, and the Freedom of Information Act. Federal policy on information culminated in the Paperwork Reduction Act of 1980 and Office of Management and Budget Circular A-130.[6]

The idea began to develop that information should be treated as a resource much like other resources such as personnel or dollars. The term *information resource management* covered a group of concepts designed to bring a new emphasis to managing information. The Report of the Commission on Federal Paperwork sought to shed light on the proper management of information when it stated that:

the real culprit of the paperwork burden is mismanagement of information resources. Government has tended to regard information as a relatively free and unlimited commodity like air or sunshine, simply ours for the asking.[7]

In an effort to implement a new way to manage information, the Paperwork Reduction Act of 1980 directed federal agencies to take a number of actions such as designating a senior official to manage information, using new policies and procedures, developing an inventory of information systems, and starting an information collection budget.

The true nature of IRM, however, has not always been clear to bureaucrats. Even today, ten years after its implementation, there is little consensus on what its core concepts are or how it is defined. One straightforward definition says that IRM is the:

planning, budgeting, organizing, directing, training, and control associated with government information. The term encompasses both information itself and the related resources, such as personnel, equipment, funds, and technology.[8]

IRM organizations and functions can pertain to anything related to information and typically include data processing, word processing, information systems, paperwork management, micrographics, records management, printing and duplicating, and library and archives.

Although in theory IRM is concerned with both manual and automated systems with paper as well as computer records, the focus has really been on computers and information systems. IRM has come to be almost synonymous with automation and computers for at least two reasons. First, over the past decade automated information systems have been by far the most visible and fastest growing component of IRM. Second, top managers in IRM organizations come more often from the ranks of computer professionals than from, for example, those of records managers, librarians, or archivists. This has turned out to be both a strength and a weakness of the IRM.

THE ROLE OF MANAGEMENT ANALYSIS IN IRM

Management analysts have been closely associated with IRM since its inception. There are a number of reasons for this aside from the fact the analysts have often dealt with information, especially in providing it to managers and decision makers. First, analysts have long been involved with automation. In addition, management analysts have frequently worked in records management and micrographics, two of the other elements that constitute IRM. Further, in some federal agencies organizational changes have actually incorporated MA units into larger IRM organizations. Recently, there has been evidence in these agencies of a trend to remove MA units from IRM organizations and have them report directly to a separate top management official. Management analysis units reporting directly to top management obviously can be more independent and objective and are less wedded to a particular technology than those organizationally located under the IRM officer.

IRM is a "natural" for management analysts and an area in which their skills are much needed and in which they can excel. One needs only to look at the goals of the Paperwork Reduction Act of 1980 to see potential roles for MA. Two of the most important goals of the act are to minimize federal cost of information handling and to ensure that ADP and telecommunications technologies are acquired and used to improve efficiency and effectiveness.

Further, the time is right to bring a stronger MA perspective to IRM. Up to this point IRM has been mainly technology driven with a strong technical ADP perspective. This is largely because ADP shops became the focal point for new IRM organizations. Now, however, with increasing cost-consciousness and a growing belief that many systems may not be worth what they cost, the focus of IRM can change from ADP and hardware to "resources" and "management" and thereby achieve greater balance. The traditional concerns of MA with information, resources, and management, make it perfectly suited to play a leadership role in IRM.

NOTES

1. Hume, Brit, "Honoring the Father of the Computer, 50 Years Late," *Washington Post*, November 26, 1990, Business Section, p. 17.

2. Rapp, William F., "Management Analysis at the Headquarters of Federal Agencies," *International Review of Administrative Sciences* 26, no. 3 (1960): 244–245.

3. Orenstein, G. S., "The True Cost of Microcomputers," *Cost Engineering* 56, no. 3 (November 1986): pp. 57–59.

4. Oman, Ray C., and Tyrone Ayers, "Productivity and Benefit-Cost Analysis for Information Technology Decisions," *Information Management Review* 3, no. 3 (Winter 1988): 31–41.

5. Ibid.

6. Caudle, Sharon L. "Federal Information Resources Management: Bridg-

ing Vision and Action," A Report for the National Academy of Public Administration, June 1987, pp. 15–27.

7. U.S. Commission on Federal Paperwork, *A Report of the Commission on Federal Paperwork*, Washington, D.C., U.S. Government Printing Office, 1977, p. 12.

8. U.S. Office of Management and Budget, *Management of Federal Information Resources, Circular No. A–130*, Washington, D.C., Executive Office of the President, December 1985, p. 3.

CHAPTER 6 _____

Organization Productivity:
A Classic Area Receives
Renewed Emphasis

Emphasis on productivity is in vogue again because of factors in the external environment of U.S. organizations. Some of these factors are the large international balance of payments deficit, the sizable federal budget deficit, increased foreign competition in both overseas and domestic markets, and the growing sense that the United States may have lost its competitive edge. If current economic trends and the attention of the mass media on productivity-related topics are any indication, the subject will be of considerable interest well into this decade.

Many of these trends seem to be altering the very fabric of the U.S. economy. These macroeconomic events are challenging U.S. organizations in new and different ways, and the level of the challenge may be higher than at any time in the recent past. The turbulence of the environment of many public and private organizations and the stiff foreign competition faced by many private firms have made productivity and performance issues a top priority.

Early in the 1980s public-sector organizations turned to private firms in their effort to increase productivity. However, with the recognition that many U.S. businesses, themselves, were proving less than competitive with foreign firms, government organizations widened their search for approaches, techniques, and tools to improve productivity. Recently, both private firms and public organizations have sought ideas from other nations, such as Japan, and have explored the potential of both qualitative and quantitative approaches.

In the past few years, through the influence of experts such as W. E. Deming, J. M. Juran, and P. B. Crosby, efforts to improve productivity have emphasized quality.[1] Improving quality is seen not only as a goal but also as the key to long-term improvements in productivity. Within many private firms and government agencies, recent concerns with quality and productivity have been placed within the rubric of "total quality management (TQM)." TQM focuses on commitment to the principle of continuous improvement, good horizontal and vertical communication in the organization, and structured problem analysis as a means to achieve fact-based decisions.

PRODUCTIVITY AND MANAGEMENT ANALYSIS

Productivity is not a new concern to management analysts. The work of Frederick W. Taylor and others in the scientific management movement was very much concerned with productivity. During the 1930s and 1940s, when the field of public administration and public management focused on the so-called principles of administration, efficiency and productivity were important goals. Much of that interest and concern carried forward to management analysis when it emerged as a distinct field in the federal government. In fact, management analysts have been involved in, if not central to, most productivity improvement efforts in the federal government over the past forty years.

As one of the core areas in management analysis, productivity is a concept with which a competent analyst must be familiar. Some aspects of productivity with which the analyst must be conversant are its assessment, measurement, and improvement. The analyst must be able to apply the classic tools from "scientific management" such as methods and time-measurement (MTM) studies, to production improvement. MTM was applied in the federal government well into the 1950s and early 1960s, when its use began to wane. Management analysts have also been involved in broader aspects of productivity efforts in the government. Three examples are the management of the Department of Defense Productivity Improvement Program, research on productivity measurement in R&D at the National Bureau of Standards in the Department of Commerce, and key involvement in the Total Quality Management initiative being carried out in many parts of the government. There are a great many other examples too numerous to mention at all levels of the executive department, from the Office of Management and Budget through the cabinet-level departments to bureau and field office organizations. Some of the specific roles management analysts perform in productivity are discussed later in this chapter.

Productivity is a natural area for management analysts to work in for a number of reasons. First, implicit to understanding productivity and certainly a requisite for improving it is the proclivity to ask the inquisitive question, "*Why?*" It is a question asked all too infrequently in most of our organizations today. For most management analysts, however, because of their inquisitive nature and because they are searchers for truth, asking why comes most naturally. A second reason is that productivity is a complex concept that requires much understanding beyond the simple productivity ratio of output divided by input. Management analysts like to solve puzzles and to figure things out. Because understanding productivity is not easy, but takes thought, research, and judgment, it fits most analysts to a tee. The last characteristic of productivity that makes it so compatible to management analysts is that it deals with both quantitative and qualitative measures. It frequently requires, for example, the ability to work with statistics as well as fluently to discuss ideas and express them in clear, concise narrative. This, again, is the forte of the general management analyst. Because management analysts are generalists, they possess the rich mix of skills to function effectively in this thought-provoking area.

The next section will delve into the topic of productivity and it will be obvious why it is so important to be able to ask those *Why* questions.

THE CONCEPT OF PRODUCTIVITY

Productivity in its strict sense is defined as output divided by input. If output increases while input stays constant, the ratio increases and productivity can be said to increase. Conversely, if input increases and output stays the same, the ratio decreases and productivity is said to decline. The productivity ratio, of course, can also be affected by simultaneous changes to both input and the output. The bottom-line measure of change in productivity is cost per unit of output—productivity increases as the cost per unit of output goes down. While the ratio of input to output is a simple way to conceptualize productivity, in most real-world applications it often hides as much as it reveals.

For the concept to be meaningfully applied, productivity normally must be defined in a broader way than as the simple input-to-output ratio. It must also be merged with, or at least related to, conceptual frameworks such as "performance," "economic return," "efficiency," "effectiveness," and "quality." First, it must be related to the marginal social or economic returns associated with outputs. Given that the goal of a private firm is to maximize profits and that the goal of a government agency is to maximize an economic or social criterion, such as net benefits or benefit/cost ratio, the marginal costs of the inputs and the marginal benefits or returns of the outputs must be considered in any meaningful measure of productivity.

Thus, issues of benefits and costs and of cost-effectiveness are intertwined with productivity. The decision to buy countable inputs for the purpose of increasing countable outputs is sound only if the value of the outputs achieved is greater than that of the inputs. For productivity to increase, the marginal benefits or profits derived from the output, not just the countable outputs, must be greater than the marginal costs of the inputs. Only when profits or cost-effectiveness increases is the purchase of additional inputs to increase outputs a sound investment decision. The measure, of course, of whether productivity has improved is a decrease in the cost per unit of output.

The fact that there are multiple inputs and multiple outputs, only some of which may be quantifiable, further complicates and adds a real-world dimension to the notion of a straightforward output/input productivity ratio. Further, economists advocating the use of "total factor productivity" suggest the inclusion of measures of all of the inputs needed to produce an output.[2] Under this approach, all inputs and all outputs should be enumerated and have a value placed on them.

Therefore, although productivity can be simplified to the ratio of output/input, the definition, quantification, and manipulation of the many factors that go into the numerator and denominator of the model can be time consuming and complex. Concepts such as performance, efficiency, and quality, to name a few, overlap and share meanings with productivity, and sometimes are used interchangeably with it.

The broadening of the concept of productivity from a simple model of countable outputs divided by countable inputs has significant advantages. If organizations are to be more competitive, effective, and efficient in producing a product or service, the concept of "improvement" must be meaningful and able to be applied usefully. The fact that concepts such as productivity and performance can overlap is in itself not negative.

PRODUCTIVITY AND THE INDIVIDUAL

Turning from the level of the organization to that of the individual and from the concept of productivity to productive behavior is a difficult transition. It appears to be quite one thing to advocate, argue for, and even generate ideas for productivity improvement at the macro, or organization, level, and quite another to make individual behavior in the work place more productive. However, if the productivity of an organization is considered to be the sum of the productivities of the individuals who compose it, improvement in productivity should start with the individual.

Perhaps the first question that should be asked is how individuals can improve productivity. Carrying this line of questioning one step further to something each of us has control over, perhaps the individual should ask, "How can I be more productive in my job?", or the corollary, "What can I do differently on my job to be more productive?" A parting suggestion for individuals who wish to do their part to help their organization, or country, through a difficult productivity crossroads might be to ask the following questions:

- How can I work smarter?
- How can others work smarter?
- How can I help others to work smarter?
- How can others help me to work smarter?
- How can I help others to help me to work smarter?

Today's management analyst should be able to approach productivity issues from a variety of directions, for example, qualitative as well as quantitative and at the micro level as well as the macro level. The next section discusses some case applications in the area of productivity.

THE ROLE OF THE MANAGEMENT ANALYST IN PRODUCTIVITY

The management analyst can play a number of significant roles in the important area of productivity. To some extent the roles analysts can fulfill are as varied as the field itself, limited only by the imagination and creativity of the analyst. Still, as one looks at the field of management analysis and at the area of productivity, a number of key roles stand out. To some degree, naturally, these roles are shaped by the particular organization and organization level of the analyst.

One common role of the management analyst is that of leader or coordinator of agency-wide or bureau-wide productivity programs. For example, most federal agencies have established productivity programs on their own initiative or in response to top management encouragement. As the name implies, the goal of these programs is to improve productivity wherever possible in the organization. Aspects of such a program may include the identification of areas for potential productivity improvement through management review or from employee suggestions; working with managers to identify specific productivity improvement objectives; measuring the trends in productivity over time; promoting the sharing of good ideas and successful approaches; managing an account set aside to provide funding for efforts that promise to improve productivity, such as a productivity capital investment fund; and reporting to top management on the progress of the program.

A second role of the management analyst in productivity programs is the conduct of periodic or ad hoc studies or inspections to identify problem areas or opportunities for improvement. The management analyst may direct the study or inspection team or simply serve as a team member. Productivity improvement studies can provide an in-depth look at factors such as mission, functions, organization structure, work methods and processes, inputs and outputs, and costs and benefits, that affect productivity.

The management analyst can also serve as a classic management consultant in the area of productivity. Managers at any organizational level can have productivity concerns. If a manager believes there is a need to improve productivity in the organization, he or she can request assistance from the head of the management analysis unit or from a particular analyst. In addition, top-level managers perceiving productivity problems or opportunities at lower levels in the organization can request the assistance of management analysts in resolving the problems or taking advantage of the opportunities. In this case, although the assistance of the analyst has been requested by top management, the analyst must develop a working relationship with the manager at the lower level, close to the problem, in order to resolve it.

A fourth role of the analyst in relation to productivity is that of an expert in the area, serving as a resource to managers who wish to increase their knowledge of productivity or to develop and apply productivity improvement principles in their own organization. In this role the analyst serves the organization by being a substantive expert. The analyst's role in productivity programs may also include responsibility for coordination and communication with other agencies sharing good ideas or developing productivity improvement efforts that call for the cooperation of two or more agencies.

The last role for the analyst in productivity to be discussed here is that of the organization "gadfly" who is ever searching for opportunities and stimulating actions to improve productivity. In this role the analyst is called on to exhibit creativity, initiative, and perseverance. Analysts should be ever vigilant for opportunities to improve organization productivity. The nature of the analyst's work in conducting studies and working with managers on problems is such that many opportunities will present themselves to the astute analyst.

CASE APPLICATIONS IN PRODUCTIVITY—
QUANTITATIVE APPROACH

It is natural to think of productivity in quantitative terms: countable outputs, such as widgets. The whole area of productivity measurement connotes something that can be counted. Measurement necessarily implies numbers and arithmetic at the low end of quantification and perhaps more-sophisticated techniques, or models, at the higher end. Part of the reason that management analysts with all of their *Why* questions add such a valuable perspective to organization productivity is that getting meaningful measures of input and output is never easy. The most obvious measures that might be used are not necessarily the best ones. Those penetrating *Why* questions often need to be asked repeatedly to arrive at the best or most meaningful measures of productivity.

A classic case of productivity deals with the introduction of new technology, frequently to replace manual processes with automation. In fact, the substitution of technology for manual processes worked so well in agricultural and industrial settings in the past that it has come to be associated with productivity improvement in the minds of most Americans. Recently, however, the effect of new technology and automation on productivity in the work place has come to be questioned. Critics argue that just because technology was associated with rapid advances in productivity in agriculture and industry at the turn of the century it does not follow that it will have a similar effect in today. They also maintain that factors other than mechanization and new technology had a major part to play in the productivity increases in the past.

The value of good productivity analysis is that it can tell the manager when an investment in new technology will increase productivity and be cost-effective and when it will not. The following productivity/cost study illustrates this point. In the 1970s an important aspect of the trend toward increasing office automation was the application of automatic typewriters and word processors to work formerly done by conventional electric typewriters. At the time the study was done a standard electric or correcting electric typewriter could have been purchased for about $700, while automatic typewriters/word processors ranged from about $5,000 to $15,000. Thus, the automated equipment cost approximately ten to twenty times as much as the conventional. Automatic typewriters were often marketed on the premise that their increased cost was more than offset by tremendously increased productivity.

One astute management analyst asked the question, "Is it possible that productivity is really increased sufficiently to offset the dramatically higher cost of the automated equipment?" This question led to the management analysis division conducting a study of the cost and productivity of the two alternative equipment configurations. The study was conducted for a sample of approximately 150 typewriters, about evenly divided between conventionals and automatics. The typing was timed, and copies of the typed output was collected and analyzed during the course of the study. In the analysis, the two cost components considered were labor cost and equipment cost. The total cost (for labor and equipment) was divided into the number of pages (and lines) typed to get a total cost per unit of output (per page or per line typed).

The study showed that although productivity of automatic type-writers was on the average 10 to 15 percent higher than of conventionals, the total cost per unit of output was much more. The reason for this, of course, was that equipment cost for the automated machines was so much higher than for conventionals. In fact, the study showed that the mean cost per typed page was about 150 percent higher on the automatics and the median cost per page about 62 percent higher. So, while the substitution of the automated equipment for the conventional did increase productivity, the increase was not nearly enough to make the new technology cost-effective compared with the conventional technology.

In a number of the organization units where the study was conducted, management accepted the new information and made changes that resulted in considerable out-of-pocket cost savings without reducing productivity. In addition, the information from the study was used for planning that resulted in better decisions on future office automation as well as cost avoidance. All this happened because one management analyst ask a variant of the *Why* question.

QUALITATIVE FACTORS IN PRODUCTIVITY

In the past, qualitative factors have not been associated with organization productivity efforts to the same degree that quantitative factors have. Recently, however, the importance of these qualitative, or "soft," factors that cannot be readily measured has received increased attention. There are at least two reasons for the current interest in qualitative factors. The first of these reasons relates to the input side of productivity, while the second pertains to the output side. There is a growing recognition that many qualitative factors go into the mix of variables that result in a productive organization. These factors include, for example, morale, the quality of interpersonal relationships, job satisfaction, and clarity of objectives, among many others.

The second reason for the emphasis on qualitative factors is that so much of the U.S. economy is now devoted to producing services rather than manufactured products. Experts increasingly doubt our ability adequately to measure value by counting outputs even when they are present. For example, determining the value of a formally published research report and the degree to which its information was transmitted informally to the scientific community prior to publication adds to the difficulty of valuation.[3] Measurement problems are compounded for organizations in which there are no quantifiable outputs or in which the output is incidental to the effect. Service-providing professions such as counseling and consulting are classic examples.

There is a recognition today that many elements go into making effective and highly productive organizations. The variables that influence productivity can be so diverse that it is necessary to focus on the broad array of areas to have maximum effect on productivity. Many of the components of the management process itself, for example, planning, organizing, directing, staffing, and evaluating, are part and parcel of productivity.

The importance of qualitative factors has most recently become evident through the emphasis on communication and leadership factors by "quality" experts such as W. E. Deming and J. H. Juran, who come from industrial engineering and operations research backgrounds. Of the three major aspects of TQM—top management commitment to continuous improvement, the establishment of structures to improve organization communication laterally and horizontally, and structured methods to analyze problems and achieve fact-based decisions—the first two are not easily measured. Indeed, leading TQM experts most often characterize their efforts to improve quality and productivity as making a "cultural change" in the organization.

TWO APPROACHES TO PRODUCTIVITY: THE CLASSICAL APPROACH AND TQM

At a minimum, there are two approaches to productivity with which today's management analyst must be familiar: the established classical approach and the now highly regarded TQM. Along with the rising interest in productivity, the approaches taken to it have changed much in recent years. In the past, a rather structured, tightly defined, and quantitative method characterized what might be called the classical approach, according to which productivity is defined as the relationship of countable inputs to countable outputs. Output is usually defined in terms of widgets, nails, reports, or pieces of paper, while input is often defined in terms of number of personnel or hours of labor. The classical approach often does not focus on intermediate outputs or "value added," or on more difficult to define inputs such as capital equipment, materials, and overhead. The classical approach is not particularly concerned with the cost of myriad and intangible inputs or the value of multiple outputs. Nor is there much concern for how one output relates to another output, or for how an output of one process becomes an input to another. In addition, the quality of the output is not of particular concern as long as it meets quantifiable specifications.

Yet, in spite of its shortcomings, classical productivity analysis was doable and often provided management with information and analysis on which to make better decisions. Advantages of classical productivity analysis were that it could be done by a well-trained, but not necessarily broadly educated, analyst, and that it provided management information in simple numerical form that could be readily digested by almost any manager. In addition, the studies needed to do classic productivity analysis could be conducted relatively easily and did not need to have direct top management involvement to provide a "vision," general direction, or strategic objectives for the organization. Further, such studies were not terribly threatening, because they involved the countable outputs that occur at various points in the work process and were seldom concerned with overall costs, benefits, profits, or the true bottom line.

The kinds of topics studied included the effect of new equipment or technology or change in work process or the number of outputs produced. One classic example is the effect of using a new date stamp on the flow of mail coming into a mail room or the effect of substituting automation for labor, for example, adding automatic typewriters or word processors in a typing pool while decreasing the number of typists. Another example is the acquisition of new equipment to reduce the amount of overtime paid or the use of temporary workers. Other common topics include work flow or process studies designed to streamline and do away with redundant procedures.

Total Quality Management takes a very different approach to productivity improvement. It was first applied on a broad scale by U.S. productivity experts working in Japan. After the astounding success of Japanese firms in world markets and the difficult competitive position of many U.S. firms, the experts who espoused TQM found a growing market for their services in the private and public sectors in the United States. Within the federal government, interest in TQM is still rising. Although it is still applied in a relatively small number of organizations, pockets of committed and successful users are proliferating.

TQM embodies many elements including assumptions, concepts, tools and techniques so that it may be thought of as having a philosophy, methodology, and means or modus operandi. A host of attributes can be used to describe TQM based on the theory and principles articulated by major proponents, such as Deming, Juran, and Feigenbaum.[4] Four of the most visible attributes of TQM as a method to improve productivity are its requirement for top management commitment to a particular set of values, the involvement of managers and workers at all levels, the use of structured problem-solving methods to achieve fact-based decisions, and the use of particular organization structures and teams. These four characteristics are discussed below.

One of the unique attributes of TQM is its requirement for top management support and participation in the quality/productivity improvement process and the need for management to make a commitment to a certain set of values. The underlying belief is that TQM cannot be achieved without management's commitment to working toward a long-term cultural change in the organization and the belief that the manager's most important job is improving the work process or system that has the potential for continuous improvement. Living by this set of values can be a traumatic change for managers who have measured their job performance by their ability to move paperwork from their in-box to their out-box.

A second characteristic of TQM is the requirement for managers and workers to work together in the quality/productivity improvement effort. While a manager's main job is to improve the work process or system, a worker is the expert in how to best perform his or her own job. Workers are encouraged "not to leave their brains at the door" but to be continuously creative and resourceful in finding ways for the organization to improve quality and productivity. Workers at all levels are considered to be a most valuable resource and essential part in TQM efforts.

Another distinctive aspect of TQM is the use of particular methodologies to document, analyze, test, and improve the work processes or systems. Both managers and workers must be trained in these methodologies because they will serve as the common ground for process improvement. The two basic methodologies of graphic charting and statistical process control (SPC) are used to measure quality and productivity and to test the process to see whether there has been any improvement. Various kinds of charting techniques are available to document the process, and different statistical methods are used to measure quality and productivity at many points in the process.

The fourth characteristic of TQM is the establishment of various structures or groups to serve as the means to carry out the methodological requirements of the approach and to improve horizontal communication in the organization. The executive steering board (ESB) is the first group that needs to be established. The ESB is composed of all top managers and is chaired by the head of the organization, be it the CEO, agency director, or commanding officer. The ESB sets the "vision" or strategic direction of the organization and must provide a high level of commitment to TQM. The next major structure is the quality management boards (QMBs) which are composed of managers and workers representing various vertical and horizontal elements of the organization. The QMBs are a permanent structure, like the ESB, and play a key role in defining the processes to be improved and in implementing changes. Process action teams (PATs) are the work groups that analyze the work process or system and propose improvements. PATs consist of representatives from the various horizontal and vertical components of the organization involved in the process. Other structures or groups may be established depending on the needs of the particular organization.

Thus, TQM, which has recently become a watchword to improving organization productivity, is based on principles and theory from various disciplines including management, behavioral science, and industrial engineering. The strength of TQM may be its interdisciplinary nature, which draws on the best of both humanistic and scientific paradigms and qualitative and quantitative disciplines to provide a holistic methodology for improving quality and productivity. As Deming's book, *Out of the Crisis* suggests, TQM may offer the last great hope of U.S. organizations in our increasingly competitive world. The management analyst who is to function effectively in today's environment must be thoroughly familiar with TQM.

NOTES

1. See Philip B. Crosby, *Quality is Free: The Art of Making Quality Certain* (New York: McGraw-Hill, 1979) and *Quality Without Tears, The Art of Hassle-Free Management* (New York: McGraw-Hill, 1984); W. Edwards Deming, *Out of the Crisis* (Cambridge: Massachusetts Institute of Technology, Center of Advanced Engineering Study, 1986); A. V. Feigenbaum, *Total Quality Control*, 3d ed. (New York: McGraw-Hill, 1983); and J. M. Juran, *Quality Planning and Analysis: From Product Development Through Use*, 2d ed. (New York: McGraw-Hill, 1980) and Juran's *Quality Control Handbook*, 4th ed. (New York: McGraw-Hill, 1988).

2. Kendrick, John W., *Understanding Productivity: An Introduction into the Dynamics of Productivity Change* (Baltimore: Johns Hopkins University Press, 1977).

3. U.S. Department of Commerce, National Bureau of Standards, *Productivity Measurement in R&D*, NBS Technical Note 890, Washington, D.C., Government Printing Office, 1975, pp. 30–33.

4. See works cited above by Deming, Juran, and Feigenbaum.

CHAPTER 7

Keys to Successful Management Analysis Studies

Management analysts perform many roles in relation to studies. Individual analysts or management analysis (MA) officers are frequently asked to conduct studies by managers and policy makers. A more-junior analyst might participate in a study as a team member, concerned, for example, with gathering particular data. If a study is small, it might be conducted by one analyst. If the study is larger or more complex, a team of analysts might be involved in the effort. Analysts are frequently asked to lead interdisciplinary teams, task forces, or other work groups. An analyst who is an expert in some aspect of management or organizations may be asked to serve as a consultant to the study team. An analyst serving as an expert resource to a study group may serve as a substantive expert in some area, such as automation, work flow, or economic analysis, or as an expert in the process or interpersonal aspects of organization interventions, such as studies.

The purpose of this chapter is to provide the keys to conducting a successful MA study. There are no simple answers to the question of how to conduct successful studies. It is a complex question that has been wrestled with in one form or another since scientific management developed before the turn of the century. More recently, the question has been addressed by the field of program evaluation which is closely related to MA. It became evident more than a decade ago that program evaluation study findings were often not accepted or implemented by managers. The study of the usefulness, acceptance, and implementation of program evaluation findings became a popular avenue of inquiry for evaluators, many of whom were academicians associated with colleges and universities. Although no clear consensus developed among evaluators about how to make their studies more useful, the program evaluation literature is a rich source of information about factors affecting the acceptance and use of study findings.[1] Some of the discussion in this chapter is drawn from that literature. It is unfortunate that program evaluators began to address problems of the acceptance and usefulness of their studies too late to prevent the weakening of the field by large federal budget cuts in the late 1970s and early 1980s. A recent GAO report shows that program evaluation funding and staffing were reduced by over a third between 1980 and 1984.[2]

Fortunately, the effects of budget cuts on MA were not nearly as drastic during that period. In fact, MA more or less held its own, although the number and quality of studies probably declined. The field changed somewhat to adapt to the rapidly changing environment, and although the number of studies probably declined, the number of management analysts in the federal government actually increased.[3] There are a number of reasons why the field of management analysis was not hurt as much as some others during the federal budget cuts of the early 1980s.

MA studies have always been more down-to-earth, practical, and decision-maker–oriented than those in fields that drew more heavily on sophisticated methodologies and had a strong academic bent. Consequently, the findings of these studies are more often accepted and implemented than those conducted in many other professional fields. For example, an analysis of the recommendations contained in the fifteen large MA studies discussed in Chapter 4 showed that about two-thirds of the recommendations were accepted wholly or in part. Although it must be kept in mind that the sample was not randomly selected, the level of acceptance is nonetheless impressive. There are a number of reasons for the usefulness of MA studies. Briefly, they are closely geared to the needs of decision makers and managers, are practical, and use straightforward methods and approaches. In addition, MA study processes are generally in tune with the culture of the organization. Let us now turn to studies, put them in context of an organization, and examine some of the keys to making them useful.

THREE TYPES OF STUDIES—VARIATIONS ON A THEME

The management analyst is involved in many types of studies. Studies can be classified into three generic types: research studies, problem-solving studies, and implementation studies. A research study is one in which the analyst is asked to collect information on a question posed by a decision maker, and its purpose is to inform. While research studies are occasionally requested, most managers are not interested in information for its own sake, but rather in using information to solve a problem or achieve an end. Indeed, research studies are often precursors of the second type of study, the problem-solving study. A problem-solving study is one in which the analyst is asked to collect and analyze information and to present one or more solutions to a problem. This type of study helps to fulfill the classic role of the management analyst in providing information and analysis to improve decision making. The third type of study, the implementation study, is one in which the analyst is asked to assist in implementing a decision that is already made. The study provides justification for or facilitates the implementation of the decision. While all studies may not fit neatly into the three-part classification scheme discussed above, the framework is a useful one for examining studies.

The most important kind of study and the one that will be elaborated on in this chapter is the Type 2 study. There are a number of reasons why studies to assist in decision making are so important. First, improved decision making is an important key to solving the problems many organizations face, and Type 2 studies are a means to improving organization decisions. Second, it is through conducting Type 2 studies that management analysts have the best opportunity to gain the experience they need to grow and to learn how to best meet the needs of their organizations. So, while some of what follows may pertain to other types of studies, it is specifically geared to the MA study to assist in decision making.

KEYS TO SUCCESSFUL STUDIES

Studies can be initiated from a variety of sources and are conducted for a wide range of reasons. First and foremost, a study is an intervention in the social system or culture of the organization. Studies are conducted amid a backdrop of the beliefs, opinions, wants, desires, hopes, and fears of the people who make up the organization. Thus, studies are more a human than a scientific endeavor. Conducting a study in a human social system is a very challenging process.

Since well-managed organizations are run as goal-seeking entities, the purpose of MA studies is not just to provide information or contribute to an organizational knowledge base, but to assist the organization in achieving its goals. The goal of the study that assesses a problem or an opportunity is to bring about the best possible decision. For example, a good MA study may recommend the most cost-effective of three management information systems (MIS) be procured. Studies also often recommend organizational change. Types of change include alterations in the behavior of individuals, in the formal policies, procedures, or rules of an organization, and in the formal organization structure and lines of authority.[4] The goal of the study, then, is to get correct action on someone's part. Good MA studies, therefore, always include either explicit or implied recommendations. And they do not always have to be recommendations for change; sometimes the best decision is to take no action.

PLANNING

One of the most important keys to a successful study is the advance thought and planning given to the study, without which the results of the study are left largely to chance. This advance thought and planning helps the management analyst both properly design the study from a technical standpoint and combat the organizational inertia and resistance that often confront studies. The time before a study is undertaken is most critical for deciding how it should be carried out.

Thinking about and planning a study should generally proceed from the general to the specific. Initially, blinders should be removed and the effort should be approached from as macroscopic a point of view as possible. Soon enough all the limitations and constraints of conducting a certain study in a particular organization will be apparent, and the effort will be off and running in a particular direction. Then it will be the management analyst's job to keep the effort moving and steer it, but changing directions will be more difficult than before the study starts when the first step can be taken in a wide variety of directions. Further, once the study starts, the analyst will be kept busy watching out for bumps, potholes, and ruts in the "road."

As many aspects as possible of the study and of the study environment should be addressed in the planning phase of the effort. Planning is necessary for the management analyst to get a good understanding of the study environment and to gather information about the host of factors that will affect it. In addition, the planning phase allows the analyst or staffer to anticipate obstacles to the study and targets of opportunity. The analyst should consider the following factors in planning an ideal study in an organization.

External Environment: If possible, choose an environment that is not too turbulent or one that favors change in the topic under study; make sure the study can be finished before a change of top management, political administration or other major environmental event.

Internal Environment: If possible, choose a tranquil environment or one that favors change in the topic chosen for study, such as cost-reduction studies in times of budget cutting; choose an organization that is nondefensive and prides itself on accepting change.

Structural Factors: Have the study initiated by the highest possible top manager; select a unit to study with a new manager who wants to make some changes; select an organization that has a history of good working relationships with the MA unit.

Behavioral Factors: Select a strong top manager to initiate the study and who will want to be involved in it; choose a decision maker who wants to make changes in the organization and with whom the analyst can establish a good working relationship; choose a decision maker who is familiar with analysis or preferably has worked as an analyst.

In reality, of course, the management analyst as an internal consultant does not normally have much control over the external environment, internal environment, or structure, but rather as the recipient of requests for studies from within the organization is usually subject to the constraints of these factors. However, these factors will change over time, and if the analyst waits, he or she may have the option of choosing the most appropriate time to do the study. The analyst who works as an external consultant ordinarily will have a greater opportunity to work in various organizations and may have more choice in selecting the organization environment that would most benefit from his intervention.

It is important to assess the external and internal environment or the structural factors of the study, even though the analyst seldom has control over them. Through assessment and planning the study can be best designed to be successful within known constraints. In particular, the locus of power surrounding the particular study should be analyzed and understood. This assessment of power relationships and organization climate allows the analyst to select the study approach, methodology, and interpersonal processes that help ensure acceptance. This aspect of planning provides input into the fourth factor, that of behavior.

Although our discussion of behavioral area follows that of the other three factors, this is no indication of its importance. Rather, it is precisely the behavioral area where the effective analyst can make the most contribution to the success of the study. The staff analyst normally has a good measure of control over behavioral factors, and the amount of control is limited only by the analyst's creativity. The more imaginative and resourceful the analyst, the more behavioral factors will be used as a lever to make the study a success. For example, the capable analyst will be creative and resourceful in establishing a good working relationship and a high level of trust with the decision maker. Further, in planning the study, the analyst can build in methods and processes that will serve to facilitate communication with the decision maker and build support for the study.

There are two components of study methodology with which the analyst should be concerned: the substantive component and the process component. The substantive component refers to the more technical aspects of the study, such as the nature of the research design and methods used in data collection, analysis, and the development of conclusions. For example, the study might include an examination of accounting reports, flowcharting, work sampling, and developing a cost analysis. The process component, on the other hand, refers to who was involved in making decisions about the conduct of the study and who carried out the various activities that constitute the study. Process also refers to how decisions were made in planning and conducting the study. For example, the process component of a particular study could be characterized by a very close working relationship between the analyst and the decision maker in the planning process. Just as no particular substantive component of a study, for example, the use of work sampling or continuous observation, is right or wrong, so no particular process component is correct or incorrect. As discussed in Chapter 8, however, getting the involvement of the decision maker is a key part of the study plan, since there is much evidence to suggest this will increase the likelihood of acceptance.

CONDUCT OF THE STUDY

The next phase is actually conducting the study. While the analyst does not control the broader contexts within which the study is conducted, he or she has considerable control over the methods and interpersonal processes used. In particular, the analyst can have an impact on personal interactions of which he or she is a part. Each of these interactions is an opportunity for the analyst to have a positive effect on the study. These interactions occur in all phases of the study, including problem definition, data collection, data analysis, and development and presentation of conclusions. Examples of interpersonal interactions associated with the study include initial interviews with decision makers, planning meetings, interviews with managers and other people in the unit being studied, and the presentation of findings. This is one reason why good interpersonal skills are so important to management analysts.

The analyst also usually has considerable control over the substantive and process methodologies referred to earlier in this chapter. During the conduct of the study the analyst carries out or implements the game plan developed during the planning phase. Although organization environments may vary as much as do individuals' personalities, the methods used in the study must be acceptable to the culture of the organization. The methods and processes need to be viewed favorably by decision makers and others involved in or affected by the study. The analyst can select from a variety of qualitative and quantitative methods and solitary and participative methodologies. For example, data can be collected in interviews, from examining statistical reports, or from experiment or actual observation. Further, the number of people conducting the study may be large or small, and these people may be organized into a team of analysts, a team composed of analysts and personnel from the unit being studied, or by some other arrangement. The number of arrangements that determine the process component of a study is limited only by one's imagination.

Although the particular study methods and processes need to be selected with the specific situation in mind, some factors associated with MA studies having a high level of acceptance include:

• being focused on a distinct rather than broad issue
• being as narrow in organizational scope as possible
• having a well-defined decision maker
• being of short duration so as to be completed before major changes in the environment occur
• having decision makers participate in defining the purpose of the study
• having decision makers informed of the progress of the study and involved in the study to the maximum extent
• having the study conducted either by a management analyst individually or by an interunit study team
• using methods of data analysis that are as straightforward and as easily understood as possible
• treating information as descriptively as possible and manipulating it as little as the problem will allow
• having the study be prospective and forward looking, rather than retrospective
• having the analyst develop recommendations sensitive to what the decision maker wants

- having decision makers participate in the development of conclusions and in reviewing draft conclusions and recommendations
- having a good number of process-oriented recommendations as well as substantive recommendations
- having an analyst who is enthusiastic about and committed to the study and who identifies with or spearheads the effort

The last phase of the study deals with formal communication of the findings to the decision maker(s) and with completion of the study. The analyst should communicate with the decision maker by the medium that is most effective in gaining acceptance for the study. The frequency and nature of communication between the analyst and the decision maker should be mutually determined. Generally, the more time the analyst can get with the decision maker the better. Following the decision maker's action on the findings, the analyst may want to ask for perceptions about the strengths and weaknesses of the study.

Finally, the analyst should bring the study to an orderly, purposeful, and positive conclusion, striving to make the decision maker's experience with the study as productive as possible. His or her future in the organization will be largely determined by his or her reputation and credibility.

GENERIC STEPS IN CONDUCTING STUDIES

Medical Science Analogy

It would be convenient for management analysts if the methods of management analysts were on a par with those of medical science. If that were the case, analysts would carry a "black bag" containing diagnostic devices to measure organizational variables such as temperature, heartbeat, and blood pressure. In addition to the basic measures of health, there would be more-sophisticated diagnostic tools for key parts of the organism such as the cardiogram, blood profile, and CAT scan. Further, there would be a well-developed procedure or book of rules for proceeding from the symptoms to the problem and to the treatment.

Although the tools of MA are not as scientific as those of medical science, the well prepared analyst has nonetheless a kit comprising a variety of tools. The intelligent and creative application of the scientific method provides the foundation for much of what the management analyst does. The generic steps of the scientific method may be thought of as building blocks in that subsequent parts are built on those already in place. For example, the symptoms that are identified lead to problem

Figure 7.1
Building Blocks

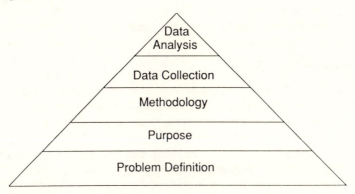

definition, the basis for defining the purpose of the study. This, in turn, leads to study methodology, which determines the nature of the data to be collected and analyzed. These building blocks are shown graphically in Figure 7.1.

Problem Definition

The definition of the problem is an essential first step in studies to assist in decision making. In many cases problem definition occurs when the management analyst is meeting for the first time with the decision maker or manager requesting the study. Organization problems are seldom simple or straightforward. Further, decision makers and managers who need assistance are frequently part of the problem and often describe the symptoms rather than the problem itself. So, the analyst is often required to work with the decision maker to develop an operational definition of the problem so it can be studied. Managers meeting with analysts to seek assistance on a problem or decision often ask questions such as: "I've heard complaints about mail not being received until two weeks after it has been received in the building. Can you see if there is any way we can speed up mailroom delivery?" or "I just finished reading an article about local area networks (LANs). I think the flow of information could be improved around here. How about conducting a study to see if we can do something about it?" or "I've been hearing through the grapevine that things aren't going well over in A Division. Conduct a review to see what we can do to improve things."

Obviously, statements such as these, while they may suggest symptoms, are not problem statements from which a useful study can be designed. It is the job of the management analyst to put on a consultant hat and work through general symptom statements, like those above, with a client until an adequate statement of problem and purpose of the study can be developed. The MA must have the skills to work with the client/decision maker to develop a good statement of the problem.

Purpose of the Study

Ideally, the purpose of the study should be well defined through close communication between the decision maker and the management analyst. It is essential to get the perceptions of the decision maker who asked for the study on what issues or topics should be addressed and resolved. Generally, the more explicit the purpose of the study the better. Here are three sample statements of study purpose:

"To improve operations in the mailroom so problems will be alleviated."

"To improve operations in the mailroom so mail will be delivered faster."

"To improve operations in the mailroom so that time-sensitive mail will be received by the responsible unit within two days after receipt in the building."

Using the simple mailroom example, it is obvious that the third statement is most effective as it focuses on the particular problem area to be addressed and has explicit criteria for success. At a minimum it is important to have a way to tell whether the purpose of the study has been achieved. In addition, the more precisely the purpose can be defined, the more the study can be targeted to focus on relevant factors. Although problem-solving studies need to strike a balance between being too narrow and too broad, studies that are defined broadly are very difficult to manage through to successful completion.

Selection of Methodology

A study methodology that best suits the purpose of the study should be selected. Generally, the management analyst has some choice over which methodology to use given the purpose of the study. The wider the range of study methods the analyst is comfortable with, the greater the flexibility in selection. As stated earlier in the chapter, methodology can be viewed in terms of substantive methodology and process methodology. The substantive methodology can either be slanted toward a scientific or a political approach, while the process methodology can be geared toward a solitary or participative approach. A scientific approach generally focuses on a definition of variables and quantification, while a political approach usually focuses on qualitative data gathered from individuals. With regard to process methodology, the

Figure 7.2
Choice of Methodologies

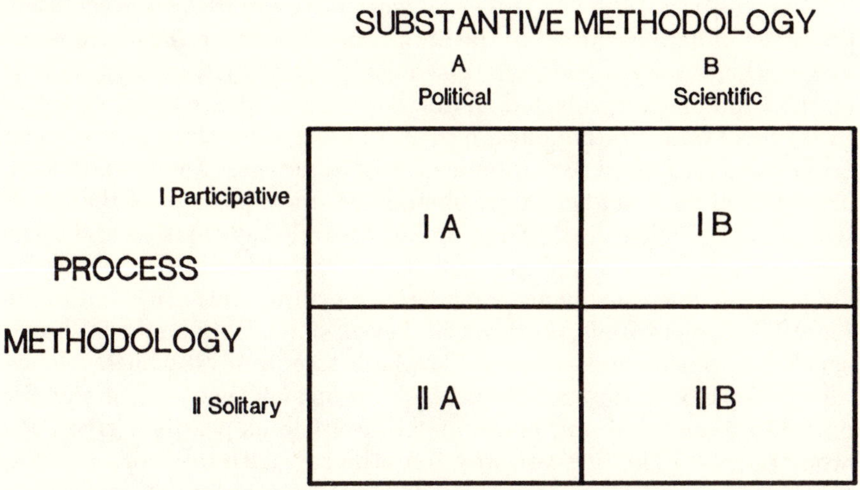

SUBSTANTIVE METHODOLOGY

	A Political	B Scientific
I Participative	I A	I B
II Solitary	II A	II B

PROCESS

METHODOLOGY

other dimension, solitary efforts generally involve a study by one person or a few people, while participative studies involve a broader sweep of people, usually as part of a study team. A simple graphic categorization of the study methodology into types A and B and types I and II is shown in Figure 7.2.

Data Collection

The type of data collected is a natural outgrowth of the choice of study methodologies. The data should serve the purpose of the study, and the more credible the data is in the eyes of the decision maker the better. Some common sources of data for MA studies are interviews, narrative reports, statistical reports, empirical data, and literature reviews. The analyst generally has a choice in selecting sources of data, even though factors such as the nature of the problem and the expertise of the analyst will limit the alternatives. Some studies, for example, cost analyses, may require quantitative data, while others, for example, organizational realignments, may require primarily narrative, descriptive, and anecdotal information. Research indicates that narrative, descriptive, and anecdotal information are more readily accepted by managers than are other kinds and that when quantitative data are used they should be accompanied by good narrative descriptive information.

Data Analysis

Data analysis refers to the organization, manipulation, and interpretation of data gathered in the data-collection phase. The data analysis methods used follow from the choice of study methodology as well as the kind of data collected. While data analysis is often thought of in terms of quantitative data, narrative descriptive data may also be organized, formatted, or summarized in some way for presentation. The kind of data analysis used should serve the purpose of the study which is to provide the decision maker credible information and analysis that can be accepted and acted on. Typical kinds of analysis includes the measurement of magnitude and intensity and the identification of trends, patterns, and exceptions. Data analysis should serve the decision maker, not the statistician or analyst who developed an elegant model. Research indicates that most decision makers prefer data to be analyzed and manipulated as little as possible, given the study purpose. The further away from the raw data the analysis goes, the more suspect it appears to many decision makers. The results of elegant statistical and economic models are often hard to interpret and are suspect in the eyes of many decision makers.

Development of Conclusions and Recommendations

The development of conclusions and recommendations is one of the most important parts of a study. In a sense, the ideas embodied in the conclusions and the recommendations are the deliverables, the products and services provided by the study. If they are good and if they are accepted and acted on, the study will likely result in benefits for the organization. After all, studies, like other functions and activities in the organization, should be cost-effective. The changes resulting from a study should result in net benefits for the organization. Sometimes, if quantifiable cost savings result, the value of the study to an organization is readily apparent. Other times, cost savings or benefits may not be readily quantifiable. Nevertheless, the goal should always be to improve the organization in some way. Because this part of the study is really the bottom line, the management analyst needs to take the utmost care to ensure that the conclusions and recommendations are technically correct, will produce net benefits for the organization in the short and long run, and will be accepted and acted on. The decision maker and his close associates need to be involved in developing or reviewing recommendations prior to the time they are formally "cast in concrete" and presented for a decision.

Figure 7.3
Continuum of Study Techniques

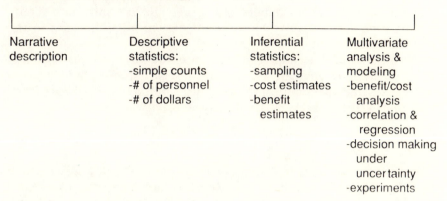

| Narrative description | Descriptive statistics: -simple counts -# of personnel -# of dollars | Inferential statistics: -sampling -cost estimates -benefit estimates | Multivariate analysis & modeling -benefit/cost analysis -correlation & regression -decision making under uncertainty -experiments |

STUDY TECHNIQUES

There are a host of techniques for use in studies for collecting and analyzing data. The techniques an analyst can use vary from the qualitative and perceptual data provided in an interview to the quantitative results of statistical and economic models. In many ways, the classic management analysis study involves the use of narrative descriptive data and data analysis techniques. Interviews are the most frequent source of data for MA studies, and conclusions and recommendations are typically developed judgmentally. Sometimes numeric data are used, and sometimes summary statistics, such as mean, median, or mode, are computed. Sometimes analysts conduct quantitatively oriented studies, such as cost and benefit analyses and the development of economic and statistical models. All in all, however, the MA study techniques are straightforward. Obviously, the use of straightforward analytical techniques does not mean that the conduct of a study is simple or that success is easy.

Recently, the competitive environment many organizations confront has brought issues of productivity, cost reduction, and efficiency and effectiveness to the fore. Studies in these topical areas require analysts to use more quantification and rigor in their studies than generally has been used in the past. There is growing demand for analysts who can conduct studies in the areas such as cost analysis, benefit-cost analysis, cost-effectiveness analysis, productivity measurement, and, in the quality area, statistical quality control. The most straightforward studies in these areas may simply involve using good analysis coupled with descriptive statistics, while more-complex studies involve using sampling and inferential statistics, present value analysis, and equations and models. Figure 7.3 represents a continuum of study techniques extending from narrative descriptive techniques on the left to multivariate analysis and modeling on the right. To meet organization needs today, management analysts should be competent not only in narrative descriptive techniques but also in all techniques in the continuum.

The purpose of this chapter is not to present a detailed discussion of the application of quantitative methods for MA studies, but rather to highlight several techniques that readily lend themselves to analysts' use. Four of these methods are discussed briefly below.

Cost Analysis

Static budgets in many public-sector organizations and declining revenues and profits in many private firms have produced a real need for MAs who can conduct cost analyses. For costs to be monitored, controlled and eventually reduced or minimized, they must first be quantified or measured. Much of this involves the same kind of analysis a prospective purchaser of a home or automobile might use. An effort is made to identify all costs related to a particular product or service over its life cycle. This provides an estimate of the magnitude of the costs and provides a simple framework for an investment decision. Getting a measure of the magnitude alone, particularly if there are hidden costs, can be an eye-opening process. Assuming this typical investment decision and that there are alternative products or services that would meet the need, cost figures are developed for each alternative. The analyst recommends one of the alternatives based on some criterion, such as lowest cost. If there is a difference in the effectiveness of the various alternatives, estimates or measures of effectiveness must be derived for each one to allow the selection of the most cost-effective alternative. Cost analysis of alternative investment choices is based on the premises of caveat emptor (buyer beware) and of comparison shopping, which smart shoppers have always used to save money.

Benefit/Cost Analysis

Benefit/cost (B/C) analysis adds an additional dimension, the benefit dimension, to cost analysis described above. With cost analysis we assume a requirement or need for the product or service to be purchased. We are willing to pay a price for the product until it becomes too terribly high. Assuming that more than one product or service are available to meet the need and they are of equal quality, we would normally choose the cheapest alternative. B/C analysis takes one step back from cost analysis and asks whether the benefits of a certain course of action or purchase outweigh the costs. For example, if we intend to procure a new management information system (MIS) to replace an existing one, will the additional benefits derived outweigh the cost?

Most of us analyze the pros and cons before making a major decision on questions such as the purchase of a house or a new car, or changing a job. Some of us even list pros and cons in an attempt to make better decisions. B/C analysis carries the process one step further by attempting to place a value on each of the pros and cons. The pros become the benefits and the cons become the costs. A dollar value is placed on as many of these itemized benefits and costs as possible. Those benefits and costs that cannot be quantified can be treated descriptively, along with political or other factors. The benefits and costs then are simply compared. For example, if the new MIS will cost $100,000 but will increase efficiency so there will be out-of-pocket savings of more than $100,000, it is obvious the benefits (or savings) will outweigh the costs. If the benefits and costs streams occur at different points in time, it is necessary to use present-value analysis to make them comparable. B/C analysis is a technique the management analyst can apply to assist management in making decisions and is particularly appropriate in times of tight resources. When the economic numbers are on the table, political and other factors can also be considered at the discretion of the decision maker.

Economic Break-Even Analysis

Managers are often interested in investments that pay good dividends, or in which a cost now can be recouped through savings or benefits in the future. The classic application of break-even analysis is one made to an investment in new and more-productive equipment. An illustration of the simplest case is the purchase of a more productive piece of equipment for $1,000 that will save $100 per month in labor cost. By dividing the out-of-pocket cost of $1,000 by the monthly saving of $100, a break-even point of ten months is computed. The shorter the break-even period, the more desirable the investment. In the real world, break-even analyses are usually slightly more complicated than in the above illustration. The initial outlay might include several cost factors in addition to the equipment itself, such as installation, maintenance, and training costs that must be computed over the life cycle of the investment. Once all of the costs and savings or benefits are identified, however, the same basic break-even model holds. Economic break-even analysis is a simple technique that can clarify issues and help the manager make cost-effective decisions.

Productivity

With the heavy emphasis on productivity in many management circles, an understanding of it is essential for management analysts. Productivity in its strict sense is defined as output divided by input. If output increases while input stays constant, the ratio increases and productivity increases. Conversely, if input increases and output stays the same, the ratio decreases and productivity declines. The productivity ratio, of course, can also be affected by simultaneous changes to both input and output. To measure productivity, of course, it is necessary to quantify both inputs and outputs. In a classic production environment, where countable outputs, such as widgets, are produced and reflect the true productivity of the organization, the basic model holds up relatively well. In most real-world organizations, however, where inputs and outputs may not be particularly obvious or may be more difficult to measure, assessing productivity may be more complex than is suggested above. This provides the perfect opportunity for the analyst who understands productivity to define, analyze, and model the inputs and outputs necessary for productivity measurement. Focusing attention on productivity, even with an imperfect model, often serves to improve it.

So, for management analysts to be really valuable to organizations today, a knowledge of some basic quantitative techniques, such as those discussed above, is essential. Analysts should be able to conduct basic cost and economic analysis, productivity and quality measurement, and statistical modeling studies. While complex issues or systems that require sophisticated analysis may require the analyst to work as middle man between the manager and the economist or statistician, the management analyst should be conversant with the terminology and concepts. The analyst who can conduct quantitative studies as well as the more general descriptive review will be in demand and will be perceived as an asset to the organization.

NOTES

1. Oman, Ray, and Bill Masters, *Implementing Change in Organizations, Based on Analysis and Evaluation Studies: A Bibliography*. Public Administration Series: Bibliography P2112. (Monticello, Ill.: Vance Bibliographies, February 1987).

2. U.S. General Accounting Office, *Federal Evaluation: Fewer Units, Reduced Resources, Different Studies From 1980*, GAO/PEMD–87–9, January 1987.

3. Interview on November 26, 1990, with Christine E. Steele of the U.S. Office of Personnel Management, Office of Workforce Information, Statistical Analysis and Services Division, pertaining to the number of management

analysts shown in the records of occupations of federal white-collar and blue-collar workers. Also see U.S. Office of Personnel Management, Federal Occupation Survey as of September 30, 1989, Table J, and the same survey for previous years.

4. Johnston, William P., and Ray C. Oman, "Overcoming Resistance to Change: Theory and Practice Provide Some Insights," *Knowledge Creation, Diffusion, Utilization* 11, no. 3 (March 1990): 268–279.

CHAPTER 8 _____

The Nature and Acceptance of Study Recommendations

The purpose of management analysis studies is to assist managers in making useful decisions. Thus the analyst is an extension of the management official and provides a product in the form of a report and a service in the form of information recommendations to managers. The purpose of the MA study, as opposed to research, is not to expand theory or knowledge but to provide solutions to problems or recommendations to achieve comparative advantage. One measure of the value of these studies is the degree to which they are accepted by management officials; a study in which many of the recommendations are accepted by the decision maker is likely to be more valuable than a study in which none or just a few are accepted.

GETTING ACCEPTANCE OF RECOMMENDATIONS— A COMMON PROBLEM

The acceptance of study findings is a concern to analysts and evaluators of all kinds, including external and internal consultants, industrial engineers, management analysts, and program evaluators. A review of the literature about factors affecting the acceptance of study findings revealed four subject areas containing relevant sources. These areas are program evaluation, management science, applied behavioral science, and organization theory, the first three of which are most closely related to the MA function in the federal government.

Since the mid–1970s, the field of program evaluation has been concerned with the use of findings, usually called "utilization" in the evaluation literature. Utilization is a special concern because of the considerable expenditure of time and dollars evaluations require. In the past decade as the program evaluation field has been forced to contract and to change its direction, it has focused on utilization even more. Although there are many differences between MA studies and program evaluations, such as scope, depth, resources required, and perspective, the evaluation literature provides useful information for all analysts and evaluators.

In part of that literature, Gary Cox uses Mintzberg's theory of management behavior to relate managerial style to the problems of implementing study findings.[1] These problems include:

1. a mismatch between the roles and styles of agency personnel and evaluators;
2. studies that are insufficiently rigorous to be convincing;
3. too much methodological sophistication and too little concern with concrete aspects of the program;
4. the fact that results are not available in time to be useful for decision making;
5. the fact that political and funding issues are often more important than evaluation results; and
6. the fact that evaluation findings are not communicated to agency personnel in ways that they can be used.

Cox also draws a number of other interesting conclusions particularly relevant to MA studies because they relate the perspective of the manager (decision maker) to that of the evaluator. First, evaluation findings are just one of several sources of information for managers' decisions and probably will be used to the extent that they are relevant to the managers' interests, which generally will be specific and concrete. Next, managers are not likely to be especially interested in issues of validity. Last, although a written report may be necessary for purposes of documentation, real communication as far as managers are concerned is oral.[2]

In the management science literature, research was conducted by Alden S. Bean and others about factors correlated with the implementation of operations research and management science (OR/MS) findings in selected business organizations.[3] Some of the major explanatory variables were the firm's operating environment, the firm's characteristics, the organizational environment of the firm's OR/MS group, the transactions between OR/MS and the organization, and the characteristics of the OR/MS group. Although the coefficients of correlation were not very high (they ranged between .1 and .5), the authors were able to identify a number of factors that were related to implementation and success.

KEYS TO STUDY ACCEPTANCE

An examination of the literature reveals many sources listing factors that affect utilization.[4] Few of the hypothesized factors, however, are examined in any detail. As Patton argues,

The issue at this time is not the search for a single formula of utilization success, not the generation of ever-longer lists of possible factors affecting utilization. The task for the present is to identify and define a few key variables that may make a major difference in a significant number of evaluations cases.[5]

Following Patton's suggestion, the approach we have taken here is to focus on a few key factors, namely, the kind of study, the nature of the recommendations, and the study methodology.

There are a number of sources in the literature that pertain directly to the kinds of efforts in which management analysts are involved. Stuart Adams, in developing a prescriptive package for evaluation research in corrections, found that "weaker" research designs were more successful in effecting organization change than were sophisticated ones. He concludes that the biggest payoffs come from weak or nonrigorous research designs, such as case studies and surveys. He notes:

Although the reasons are not fully understood, some hypotheses may be stated: (a) these non-rigorous research designs fit into the decision-making styles and needs of administrators; (b) there is greater pressure on corrections for systems improvement than for client improvement; (c) in times of rapid change, conditions are not favorable for the use of strong research designs; and (d) correctional administrators have not yet supported rigorous design to the extent required to make them generally effective.[6]

In addition to the research design aspect of methodology, the degree of decision-maker participation in the study is another area discussed in the literature. A study by Waller and others places user involvement in the forefront.[7] The report concludes that "the only characteristic of an evaluation system associated with utility was the degree of involvement of the user in an evaluation activity."

Mark Van de Vall has done research on the effect of methodology and user participation on utilization of applied social science and social policy findings. Van de Vall and Bolas concluded that:

The impact of social policy research upon organizational decisions is higher when the research sponsor and research consumer are identical or closely linked, rather than consisting of two separate and independent organizations; and projects of social policy research accompanied by a steering committee consisting of representatives from the research team, the research sponsor, and research consumer(s) tend to score higher on policy impact than projects lacking a steering committee.[8]

Van de Vall, Bolas, and Kang examined the effect of methodology on the use of research findings in the area of industrial and labor relations in the Netherlands. Some of their conclusions useful to the management analyst are:

The use of qualitative methods in applied social research leads to a higher impact upon industrial policy making than using quantitative methods, particularly tabular analysis.

The more the methodological mixture of applied research favors qualitative methods, the more intensively the projects are utilized in company policies.[9]

The literature cited here provides a framework for management analysts for thinking about the acceptance and use of their study results. Although the above research was conducted primarily by program evaluators, it is directly relevant to MA and to other fields, such as industrial engineering, operations research, and program analysis, concerned with conducting studies to assist in decision making.

ANALYSIS OF RECOMMENDATIONS FROM MANAGEMENT ANALYSIS STUDIES

This chapter analyzes the recommendations from MA studies described in Chapter 4 and provides insight into the nature and acceptance of study findings.[10] Although the literature provides considerable discussion of the broad factors affecting utilization, few studies discuss the details of individual recommendations and therefore may not be probing deeply enough.[11]

A CLASSIFICATION OF STUDY RECOMMENDATIONS

All fifteen of the MA studies examined made recommendations. The number of recommendations varied from study to study, ranging from 2 to 33. For the fifteen studies there were a total of 172 recommendations, or an average of 11 per study. The recommendations naturally cover a wide range of topics and were classified on the basis of three categories: subject content, scope, and type (content or process) (see Table 8.1).

Subject Content

The 172 recommendations were classified by one of twelve subject content areas. The most common subject of recommendations was that of work methods and procedures with forty-eight of the total, followed by management systems with thirty-seven. There were twenty-four and twenty-nine recommendations pertaining to organization structure and functions and policy, respectively. Eighteen recommendations pertained to delegations of authority and responsibility, while a smattering of recommendations fell into the other categories.

Scope of Recommendations

The second category dealt with the scope of recommendations. The term *scope* pertains to the breadth in terms of the number of organization units affected by the recommendation. Thus scope is a surrogate term for the number of people affected. Ten different subcategories of size were defined, ranging from that of section to that of an entire cabinet-level department. The largest single subcategory included sixty-six of the recommendations and pertained to programs that cut across organization unit lines within a bureau. Thirty-four recommendations pertained to entire bureaus, while thirty-one recommendations dealt with major operating units composed of more than one division. Nineteen recommendations dealt with an entire department, while seventeen pertained to individual divisions, and a much smaller number to lower-level units.

Type of Recommendations

Recommendations were designated as either pertaining to content or process. Content recommendations propose substantive change, while process recommendations propose further study. The vast majority of recommendations, 94 percent, pertained to content.

ACCEPTANCE OF RECOMMENDATIONS

Information about the acceptance of recommendations was gathered in interviews with the management analysts who conducted the studies. Acceptance of recommendations is not the same as implementation. Acceptance pertains to the oral or written acknowledgement of acceptance by the decision maker. Actual implementation of a recommendation, of course, was considered evidence of acceptance. Each recommendation was reviewed, discussed with the interviewee, and considered to be accepted, partly accepted, or not accepted.

Table 8.1
Characteristics of Individual Recommendations

							S T U D I E S									Total	
A. Subject content	A	B	C	D	E	F	G	H	I	J	K	L	M	N	O	Number	Percent
1. equipment and hardware technology																0	0
2. work methods and procedures	2	6	5			3	11		1	1	9	3	2	5		48	28
3. Job/position structuring											3					3	2
4. organization structure and functions	3		1	3		11		2	1		1	1		1		24	19
5. policy	1	6			2	7	7		3		3					29	16
6. personnel, staffing level				2											1	3	2
7. training											4				1	5	3
8. physical place (or space)																0	0
9. delegation of authority or responsibility	6		2								10					18	10
10. interpersonal behavior																0	0
11. management systems	4		1	2		12	12						2		4	37	21
12. program/budget							2		2					1		5	3
																172	

							S T U D I E S									Total	
B. Scope: number of people or organization units affected	A	B	C	D	E	F	G	H	I	J	K	L	M	N	O	Number	Percent
few – 1. section																0	0
2. branch				2												2	1
3. division			7										3	7		17	10
4. program	7	25						12	9		13					66	39
5. major operating unit										3		25			6	34	20
6. bureau							31									31	18
7. more than one bureau																0	0
8. department (agency)			7			12										19	11
9. one office unit						2										2	<2
10. outside agency														1		1	<1
																172	

STUDIES

	A	B	C	D	E	F	G	H	I	J	K	L	M	N	O	Total Number	Percent
C. Type:																	
1. content	5	20	7	7	2	12	31	12	9	2	13	24	4	7	6	161	94
2. process	2	5					2			1		1				11	6
D. Complexity:																	
1. low	1	10	3		2	3	8	11	3		4	4		4	3	56	33
2. medium	4	14	4	4		7	15	1	6	2	7	21	2	3	2	92	53
3. high	2	1		3	2	2	10			1	2		2	1	1	24	15
E. Specificity:																	
1. low	2	11		1	1	1	6	1	2		11	6	3	1		31	18
2. medium	3	12	5	6		9	20	11	7	3		19	1	5	6	20	69
3. high	2	2	2		2	2	7				2		1	1		21	13
F. Degree of Change from Status Quo:																	
1. low	5	10	2	1	1	8	6	7	1		1	8	1	3	3	42	24
2. medium	5	14	5	2	1	16	16	5	8	3	8	15	1	4	1	96	55
3. high	2	1		5		4	11				4	2	3		2	34	21

115

There was much variation from study to study concerning the degree to which recommendations were accepted (see Tables 8.2 and 8.3). Overall, of the 172 recommendations, 117 were accepted, 44 were not accepted, and 11 were partly accepted. Five studies, ranging in size from two recommendations to twenty-five recommendations, had all recommendations accepted. Two studies with seven and twelve recommendations respectively had none accepted. The remaining eight studies had some recommendations accepted and some not accepted. Four studies had partly accepted recommendations.

RELATIONSHIPS BETWEEN KINDS OF RECOMMENDATIONS AND LEVEL OF ACCEPTANCE

In an effort to understand more about factors affecting study acceptance, this section examines the relationship between the kind of recommendation and the level of acceptance. The relationship between kind of recommendation and level of acceptance is examined recommendation by recommendation on the basis of the typology presented earlier in this chapter. This more detailed analysis by individual recommendation provides additional insights into factors affecting the acceptance of recommendations (see Table 8.4).

Subject Content

The subject content of recommendations category is divided into nine subcategories representing a range of subjects. There is considerable variation in level of acceptance among the subject content areas. All of the recommendations pertaining to job/position restructuring, personnel staffing levels, program and budget, and training were accepted. The next highest category was management systems/work systems, where 78 percent of the recommendations were accepted, followed by the category of work methods and procedures with a 73 percent acceptance. Sixty-one percent of the recommendations concerning delegations of authority, somewhat less than average, were accepted. The two kinds of recommendations with the lowest level of acceptance were those of policy (51 percent) and organization structure and functions (46 percent).

The wide variation in the level of acceptance suggests that the subject of recommendations affects acceptance. It has been hypothesized that recommendations on procedures are less fundamental and far-reaching than those on organization structure and functions and policy and are therefore more readily accepted. Our data substantiate this hypothesis.[12]

Table 8.2
Number of Recommendations Accepted

Recommendations:								S T U D I E S									
	A	B	C	D	E	F	G	H	I	J	K	L	M	N	O	Total	Percent
Total Number	7	25	7	7	2	12	33	12	19	3	13	25	4	7	6	172	
Number:																	
Accepted	2	22	3	-	2	-	24	12	4	3	8	25	1	7	4	117	68
Partly Accepted	2	-	2	-	-	-	4	-	3	-	-	-	-	⊦	-	11	6
Not Accepted	3	3	2	7	-	12	5	-	2	-	5	-	3	-	2	44	26

Table 8.3
Percentage of Recommendations Accepted

S T U D I E S

Percent of Recommendations:	A	B	C	D	E	F	G	H	I	J	K	L	M	N	O	Average Percent
Accepted	29	88	42	-	100	-	73	100	44	100	61	100	25	100	66	62
Partly Accepted	29	-	29	-	-	-	12	-	33	-	-	-	-	-	-	5
Not Accepted	42	12	29	100	-	100	15	-	23	-	39	-	75	-	34	33

Table 8.4
Relationships Between Kind of Recommendation and Level of Acceptance

Column groups A–O each contain three sub-columns: A (Accepted), P (Partially Accepted), N (Not Accepted). Totals and percentages follow.

	A			B			C			D			E			F			G			H			I			J			K			L			M			N			O			Total Acc	Total Part	Total Not	Total	% Acc	% Part	% Not
	A	P	N	A	P	N	A	P	N	A	P	N	A	P	N	A	P	N	A	P	N	A	P	N	A	P	N	A	P	N	A	P	N	A	P	N	A	P	N	A	P	N	A	P	N							
A. Subject content																																																				
1. work methods and procedures	1	-	1	5	-	1	2	2	1							-	-	3				11	-	-	1	-	-	1	-	-	6	-	3	3	-	-	-	-	2	5	-	-				35	2	11	48	73	4	23
2. job, position restructuring																																														3	-	-	3	100	-	-
3. organization structure and functions				3	-	-	-	-	1	-	-	3							4	3	4				-	1	1	1	-	-	1	-	-	1	-	-				1	-	-				11	4	9	24	46	17	37
4. policy	-	1	-	4	-	2							2	-	-	-	-	7	6	-	1	1	-	-	1	-	-				1	-	2	1	-	1	1	-	1							15	1	13	29	51	3	45
5. personnel, staffing level																																		1	-	-										3	-	-	3	100	-	-
6. training				6	-	-																									4	-	-													5	-	-	5	100	-	-
7. delegation of authority or responsibility				6	-	-				-	-	2				-	-	2	1	-	1	3	2	1													1	-	-							11	2	5	18	61	11	28
8. management systems	1	1	2	4	-	-	-	-	1	-	-	2				11	-	1	2	-	-													10	-	-				2	-	-	2	-	2	29	2	6	37	78	6	16
9. program/budget																												1	-	-	2	-	-	2	-	-										5	-	-	5	100	-	-
B. Scope: number of people or organization units affected																																																				
few – 1. one official unit													2	-	-				2	-	-																									2	-	-	2	100	0	0
2. branch													2	-	-																															2	-	-	2	100	0	0
3. division				22	-	3	3	2	2																						1	-	2	1	-	2	7	-	-							11	2	4	17	65	12	23
4. program																						12	-	-	8	-	-	8	-	-	8	-	5	25	-	-										58	-	8	66	88	0	12
5. major operating unit	2	2	3																22	4	5	12	-	-	4	3	3																4	-	2	22	5	7	34	65	15	20
6. bureau										-	-	7				-	-	12																												22	4	5	31	71	13	16
7. department (agency)																																					-	-	1							-	-	19	19	0	0	100
8. outside agency																																														-	-	1	1	0	0	100
C. Type:																																																				
1. content	-	2	3	17	-	3	5	-	2	-	-	7	2	-	-	-	-	12	22	4	5	12	-	-	4	3	2	2	-	-	8	-	5	24	-	-	1	-	3	7	-	-	4	-	2	106	11	44	161	66	7	27
2. process	2	-	-	5	-	-													2	-	-				1	-	-				1	-	-													11	-	-	11	100	0	0

119

Scope of Recommendations

The second category pertained to the scope of recommendations and is concerned with the number of organization units affected. It can be hypothesized that the smaller the scope, that is, the fewer organization units affected, the greater the probability of recommendations being accepted. Among the eight organization levels examined, there was wide variation in the degree of acceptance. The recommendations pertaining to one office and branch-level units were all accepted. Divisions and major operating units (composed of more than one division) each had about 65 percent of the recommendations accepted. Recommendations about specific programs had an 88 percent level of acceptance, while 71 percent of the recommendations on bureau-wide issues were accepted. None of the recommendations directed at department-wide issues was accepted.

Viewing the level of recommendation acceptance from the smallest scope to the largest, the data suggest the tendency for recommendation acceptance to decrease as the size of the organization and the number of units affected increase, particularly at the extremes. It should be noted, however, that divisions, major operating units, and bureaus all had about the same level of acceptance. Subcategory five, program level units, is different from the other subcategories because programs are specific missions that cut across formal organization boundaries. The focus on common program goals may account for the relatively high acceptance for program recommendations.

Type of Recommendation

The last category concerned the content or process nature of recommendations. Content recommendations propose specific substantive actions or solutions, while process recommendations propose that a certain process, often further study, be carried out. Decision makers accepted all of the process recommendations, while 66 percent of the content recommendations were accepted. The explanation for this may be that the specific, definite nature of content recommendations can be more threatening in organizations than a proposal to pursue an approach or process.

MANAGEMENT ANALYSTS' COMMENTS ABOUT FACTORS THAT AFFECTED ACCEPTANCE

Each management analyst interviewed was asked, "What factors affected the acceptance of recommendations?" The researcher frequently followed this open-ended question with probing questions to

elicit information from the analyst about factors that affected acceptance for his or her particular study. A wide variety of issues were
mentioned, including external environment, organization climate, and
aspects unique to a particular study. In the following paragraphs the
more general issues are discussed first, followed by items special to a
particular study. Paraphrases and anecdotal style are used to help
convey the flavor of the interviews.

These MA studies were all conducted in the federal government, and
change of political administration was mentioned as adversely affecting acceptance. A number of studies were started in one administration
and completed in another. One analyst indicated that with the change
of administration the viewpoints of top management and the working
environment changed and there was less general support for the study.

Several factors in the external organization environment aided the
conduct of successful studies. One analyst described the external environment surrounding his study as exerting a great deal of pressure.
The study concerned a subject that was brought up in congressional
confirmation hearings, thus putting pressure from outside the agency
itself on the department secretary and under secretary. The analyst
concluded that the existence of this external pressure helped the acceptance of recommendations.

The leader of one study said that both the organization environment
and factors related to the study itself favorably affected acceptance.
The level of consensus within an organization about the significance
of the problem under study has implications for decision makers' will-
ingness to take action. The analyst described the problem in saying
that the general seriousness of the problem helped acceptance. For
example, the department under secretary was dedicated to being responsive, and he recognized the need for a strong administrative system. In addition, prompting of the agency by Congress and the U.S.
General Accounting Office may have helped. Some specific factors
about the study itself, such as the careful selection of study group
members, may have aided the study. The process by which the group
worked involved getting agreement among members on the problem
and solutions. When there is consensus about the problem, efforts to
produce acceptable recommendations are facilitated. Within the group,
recommendations were kept general enough that agreement could be
maintained.

The existence of more than one client or a lack of clarity of the
identity of the real client were factors cited as affecting acceptance.
One analyst indicated that the presence of two levels of clients, both
of whom must decide on the acceptability of recommendations, made
gaining acceptance difficult. This was particularly true when lower
organization levels initiated studies and final approval authority

rested with higher-level decision makers. In this case the same person who initiated the study did not have authority to give final approval. Higher management was usually less involved in the study and was less supportive even though these officials were responsible for final approval.

The organization's climate and culture were also cited as affecting acceptance of recommendations. One analyst felt that there is a sincere desire within his bureau to improve responsiveness to clients, a real sense of mission that is shared. Substantive improvements to real problems were proposed in the study. The study unearthed real issues and problems that management was willing to deal with because of shared concerns.

In one agency the analyst indicated the study came about and was facilitated by personnel changes. The new division director was very receptive; he had no vested interest. The study allowed him to make changes he felt were needed and to increase his management control. He believed he would come under pressure to reduce the number of personnel in any case. The study recommendations served to justify the changes that had been made. Increased workload made procedural changes easy to sell. There was low morale in the office, and the new director felt changes would improve it.

In addition to the remarks above, analysts also commented on a number of factors directly related to the studies, including such matters as the initiator of the study, support group and power relationships, and the study methods and process.

The leader of one study team believed that high-level initiation of his study and an open communication climate facilitated the study's acceptance. The commissioner of the agency agreed to the study. The study team never made personalities an issue. It tried to show the unit being studied what it was doing. The project liaison person could attend study team meetings. The group under study never felt "we were trying to pull something." The study team tried to establish an open climate and an openness in communication.

Regarding the importance of the initiator of the study, one analyst observed simply that experience had shown that studies initiated in the MA unit itself had a low level of acceptance. On the other hand, when studies are requested, the requestor is ready to look at the recommendations and alternatives. One analyst indicated that a difference in perceptions about the purpose of the study affected acceptance. Some people felt the rule-making process was being broadened to involve too many parts of the organization. There was a difference of perception about whether the proposed changes were needed. According to one perception the study was done for the office that requested it and tailored to meet its view. A few offices believed their views were not articulated in the study. Workload constraints also had an effect; some recommendations involved additional work.

A number of analysts suggested that intraorganization support groups and power relationships were key factors affecting acceptance. The development of a support group during the course of the study aided the acceptance of findings, according to one analyst. At the same time support groups developed, groups opposing the study emerged. In the view of another analyst the most important factor affecting acceptance was that of organizational power relationships. According to the analyst, the forces against the study were too strong for forces favoring it. An analyst involved in a large-scale study indicated that power in the form of union pressure and the limitations it had placed on the decision makers' options affected the study. The analyst felt that a strength of the study was the fact that recommendations were developed in a systematic way. The union became a legitimate actor because its membership could be affected by the study recommendations.

In one MA study the team leader indicated that factors concerning the study itself affected acceptance. He said that the MA unit had the facts, had done its homework, and it had more information to bring to bear on arguments. It had an in-depth understanding of the current system. Once the study made the problem of wasted dollars explicit, recommendations for improvement became acceptable. Once the problem became evident, people knew follow-up audits would make the bureau look bad if nothing was done.

An analyst who conducted a large study himself cited a number of factors specific to the study as affecting acceptance. First, there was an explicit interpretation of the data. The use of a 100 percent sample lent credibility to the study. Further, some top managers had prejudices confirmed by the results. The data in the report was also in the computer—the use of a common data base may have added credibility. Last, the study responded to what the decision maker wanted to know.

An analyst on one study team made many observations about a variety of political and personal factors that helped produce a favorable reception for his study. Program officials liked the recommendations. The people in Washington, D.C., did not get blamed; it was a field responsibility. Problems were field-related, not headquarters-related, so headquarters officials could accept them. The use of quarterly status reports on the recommendations may have helped acceptance. The study showed the program was better than many people thought it was, so favorable information was presented. The program manager was a technical type and was simply interested in improving the program. He was not a political actor and was glad the concept of the program was validated by the study. The program manager had a bigger problem; the regional directors wanted to abolish his program.

DECISION MAKERS' VIEWS ON FACTORS
AFFECTING ACCEPTANCE

Interviews were also conducted with managers and decision makers who were recipients of the fifteen large MA studies considered in this research. The interviewees included political appointees and senior career government officials. In the interviews, decision makers and managers expressed views about factors they believed influenced the acceptance of study recommendations. These factors covered a wide range of variables including external environment, organization climate, and items unique to a particular study. This discussion proceeds from more-general to more-specific factors associated with the study itself.

Factors in the environment external to the organization where the study was conducted were mentioned as affecting acceptance. One program manager commented that studies done just before a change of political administration face the risk of personnel and policy changes that could adversely affect recommendations acceptance. The manager believed this is more true for studies involving programs than for those concerned with administrative management issues. In another case, changes in organization structure and in personnel were observed to dampen enthusiasm for some recommendations.

Occurrences in the external environment were also cited as facilitating the acceptance of recommendations. For example, external pressure, such as from the U.S. General Accounting Office or Congress, was said to make decision makers inclined to take action on a problem. In addition, the role of House and Senate reports, review commissions, and pressure from Congress on studies was considered to be important in decision makers' accepting recommendations.

One program manager commented that the number of organization units affected by recommendations influences acceptance. When a program that cuts across organization lines is studied, more people have to agree for acceptance to be achieved. Organization design also can have an impact. With some forms of program and matrix management, people who have a role in the program are not under the control of the program manager.

One decision maker evaluated study recommendations on the basis of their effect on the organization as a whole. His criteria for acceptance included:

- the short- and long-term impact on operations, including disruptions to existing operations;
- the impact on workers, first-level supervisors, and second-level supervisors;
- the cost;

- the time it will take to implement;
- the impact on people, staffing, and pay structure;
- the effect on productivity; and
- the interrelationships of the part to the whole.

Although decision makers obviously remarked on factors in the external environment and the larger organization that affected acceptance, the majority of observations pertained to various aspects of the study including content, process, and presentation of findings, among others.

What One Decision Maker Liked About a Study

One program manager cited many factors related to a study that made him favorably disposed to the recommendations. He liked the study because it asked, "How can we improve the program?" Recommendations designed to improve a program are easy to accept. Some specific factors the manager believed favorably affected acceptance were the facts that:

- it was clear who the leader of the study was and that he controlled the study;
- the study was handled smoothly, and the personality of the leader was compatible with that of the program people;
- the study was seen as an opportunity to help the program manager achieve what he wanted; it gave third-party support for things the program managers wanted to do;
- the study was handled very professionally; the study team was able to put the program manager and other program people at ease;
- it was an open-minded, fact-gathering study;
- the team leader was open and honest;
- the study team went to the source to get information; team members conducted many interviews;
- the study team leader created an atmosphere that this was a serious study; the team was not just going through the motions; if the study showed the program to be good, it would have top management support;
- the conceptual framework of the study and the analysts gave new insights to the program manager;
- the study report was used as a management tool; for example, it was widely distributed; it was a bible in the field;
- the use of the concepts of cost-effectiveness and productivity were new ideas the program people latched on to;
- the study made use of a variety of methods, both quantitative and qualitative;

• the report was very readable; you did not need to be a technical expert to understand it; and

• the study did not disrupt program operations.

Another factor that affected the acceptance and implementation was the use of a procedure to follow up on recommendations in the study.

Decision Makers' Concern with the Substance of the Study

The comments listed above embody many of the aspects of studies that were considered to affect recommendations' acceptance. These include study method and process and personal and credibility factors. However, substance or content of the recommendations was cited most frequently as a factor affecting acceptance. One policy maker commented that the decision maker is not much concerned with process questions such as "How it was decided how the data would be analyzed." To him the content of conclusions and recommendations was the important thing.

Another decision maker indicated that there is no particular concern with methodology as long as it is generally appropriate. A second manager suggested that the decision maker is more concerned with results than with methodology. He generally examines methods when the findings do not fit his intuition.

Yet another decision maker commented that a major factor affecting acceptance was how well the recommendations and their implications were understood. The depth and breadth of thought that went into the development of the recommendations in addition to the way the recommendations were presented to decision makers affect acceptance. The most important factor was the content of the recommendations.

One manager explained that because content is most important, it is the part of the study decision makers are asked to respond to. The recommendations discuss content, not methods, so content is considered first. Concern with methodology comes after concern with content, but if the methodology is particularly sound a recommendation might be harder to refute.

Managers also discussed a number of specific characteristics of recommendations that favored acceptance. One program manager mentioned that he welcomed recommendations that would improve efficiency and reduce paperwork, streamline operations, and provide an opportunity to get some of his ideas accepted. Heavy workload and a shortage of personnel help to make efficiency recommendations acceptable. Further, the fact that some of the recommendations came from the unit under study facilitated their acceptance. The face validity of recommendations, of course, increases the probability of acceptance. When recommendations deal with less-sensitive issues and not with the most controversial areas, acceptance is aided. The fact that the recommendations were about less-major and more easily dealt with issues increased acceptance.

Another manager commented that one study recommendation was to hold a meeting in the loan servicing area. This was not a threatening recommendation, and such a meeting was a long-standing desire for many people. The manager gave criteria for acceptance. The recommendations should be things the manager can pick up and use and should be implementable without further study. Last, for recommendations to be accepted, the organization must be ready for them.

Some interviewees felt "the facts spoke for themselves." Decision makers' belief in objective information was articulated by one interviewee who thought the outside, third-party viewpoint of MA helped the acceptance of recommendations. He believed the specific content information about workload and staffing provided in the study was the most important factor affecting acceptance of recommendations.

Decision Makers' Concern with Study Methods

Despite decision makers' stated interest in study content, many of their comments reflected a concern with study methodology and various other factors. For example, a number of decision makers commented on the use of study teams. Several expressed a preference for the use of study teams composed of people from throughout the organization in order to get diversified thinking and to help implement recommendations. A study-team approach yields better study content as well as better implementation. Another manager felt that recommendations stand a better chance of acceptance if the study was done by an objective third party and that the use of an interunit task group takes longer and may not produce a better result.

Some decision makers also displayed a concern about study method and process through their guidance and supervision of analysts during the course of the study. Others commented on what they considered to be a good study methodology and process. One interviewee noted that rather than using a statistical sample, the team collected data from 100 percent of the stations, thus increasing credibility.

More generally, one manager stated that as long as the report is written in plain English, the methodology can be as complex as necessary to be sound. Professionalism is important, but the details of the methodology should be put in the appendix of the report. In addition, a policy maker observed that studies should follow the steps of scientific problem solving. Studies should be orderly, and recommendations should come after the data are analyzed. Yet another decision maker indicated there was not much analysis of the interview data collected in a study and that this helped the recommendations' acceptance. Information was presented in the report much as it was collected from the source. Information is often overanalyzed in reports.

A number of interviewees also discussed the importance of communication and of presentation of findings. One manager indicated the importance of communication with key people and the support of people such as division chiefs in having study recommendations accepted. Frequent interactions with decision makers were considered to help the study's acceptability. One interviewee commented that it is important for decision makers to be informed of the progress of a study; there should be some interaction along the line. The presentation of the recommendations orally and in writing in a form appropriate to the audience is a factor affecting their acceptance.

Another factor mentioned by several decision makers was credibility or "the personal factor." One decision maker, for example, stated explicitly that the credibility of the person doing the study was the most important factor in the acceptance of recommendations. Credibility was defined in terms of academic credentials, experience, common sense, real-world versus theoretical knowledge, and an understanding of what is achievable and what is not. Similarly, a top policy maker indicated that decision makers' perception of the analyst conducting the study— his breadth and understanding of the organization environment— made recommendations more acceptable. Thus, the reputation of the analyst is very important. Another decision maker remarked that input from managers who were interviewed during the course of the study lent credibility to the recommendations. Therefore, both the methods used and the individual who conducted the study could affect the credibility of the effort.

Several other comments about factors affecting acceptance were mentioned by decision makers. They include:

- If tables are used they should be analyzed in the narrative and the findings summarized.

- By and large, analysts should attempt to deal with the political ramifications of their studies.

- Analysts should inform decision makers of any findings that might be surprising.

- An important objective for analysts and for the study is to educate the manager.

- An important criterion for the acceptance of recommendations is that they fit the context of the organization's culture and climate.

- Methodology is not as important as the question of who contributed the information and whether the appropriate people were contacted.
- Many decision makers like to have both empirical data and opinions.
- Cost issues are interesting and useful to the decision maker.
- Acceptance is facilitated if top management's perceptions are confirmed by the study.
- To gain acceptance for recommendations it is important that a key decision maker "buy in" and serve as the "point" for the study. "Decision maker must be comfortable with it."

A factor that has been discussed in the literature is that of providing the study on time. One interviewee stated pointedly that the study should be done in two or three months: "That is all that management will tolerate—immediate results."

A SUMMARY OF FACTORS INFLUENCING ACCEPTANCE

Many of the above variables operate individually while others work in concert with a myriad of other factors. The following kinds of studies had lower than average acceptance of recommendations:

- studies of large-scale questions;
- studies that took considerable time to complete, for example, two years or more;
- studies conducted in isolation from the organization unit(s) studied;
- studies that used sophisticated methodologies;
- studies initiated by a decision maker at one level but needing approval by a decision maker at another level;
- studies that did not have clear focus or clients;
- studies that were begun in one political administration and completed in another;
- studies that proposed changes to fundamental organization structure, functions, and policy.

Recommendations from the following kinds of studies had higher than average acceptance:

- studies that presented information from people in the unit studied in the same form in which it was presented to the analysts, without extensive manipulation of data;
- studies that were able to build in rewards to the people in the unit studied and to unit managers, for example, presenting their ideas in the report;

- studies that were done with much interaction between the people doing the study and people from the area studied;

- studies conducted by an individual analyst rather than by a team consisting solely of analysts;

- studies conducted by an interunit study team composed of analysts and people from the unit being studied;

- studies that presented new ideas about which managers in the unit studied became enthusiastic;

- studies that evidenced considerable agreement about the nature of the problem and its importance.[13]

NOTES

1. Cox, Gary B., "Managerial Style: Implications for the Utilization of Program Evaluation Information," *Evaluation Quarterly* 1, no. 3 (August 1977): 499–509.

2. Ibid.

3. Bean, Alden S., Michael Radnor, and David A. Tansik, "Structural and Behavioral Correlates of Implementation in U.S. Business Organizations," in *Implementing Operations Research and Management Science,* Randall L. Schultz and Dennis P. Slevin, eds. (New York: American Elsevier Company, 1975), pp. 115–119.

4. Oman, Ray, and Bill Masters, *Implementing Change in Organizations, Based on Analysis and Evaluation Studies: A Bibliography* (Monticello, Ill.: Vance Bibliographies, February 1987).

5. Patton, Michael Q. et al., "In Search of Impact: An Analysis of the Utilization of Federal Health Evaluation Research," in *Using Social Research in Public Policy Making,* Carol Weiss, ed. (Lexington, Mass.: Lexington Books, 1977), p. 142.

6. Adams, Stuart, *Evaluative Work in Corrections: A Practical Guide,* U.S. Department of Justice, Washington, D.C., Government Printing Office, March 1975, p. 115.

7. Waller, John D., John W. Scanlon, Don M. Kemp, and Paul G. Nalley, *Developing Useful Evaluation Capability: Lessons from the Model Evaluation Program,* U.S. Department of Justice, Washington, D.C., Government Printing Office, June 1979, p. 11.

8. Van de Vall, Mark D., and Cheryl Bolas, "The Utilization of Social Policy Research: An Empirical Analysis of Its Structure and Functions," 74th Annual Meeting of the American Sociological Association, Boston, August 27–31, 1979.

9. Van de Vall, Mark D., Cheryl Bolas, and Tai S. Kang, "Applied Social Research in Industrial Organizations: An Evaluation of Functions, Theory, and Methods," *The Journal of Applied Behavioral Science* 12, no. 2 (April-May-June 1976): 172–173.

10. Oman, Ray C., "The Nature, Conduct, and Acceptance of Management Analysis Studies in Civilian Federal Agencies," unpublished doctoral dissertation, The George Washington University, Washington, D.C., 1983.

11. Johnston, William P., Jr. and Ray C. Oman, "Overcoming Resistance to Change: Theory and Practice Provide Some Insights," *Knowledge Creation, Diffusion, Utilization,* 11, no. 3 (March 1990): 268–279.

12. Ibid.

13. Oman, Ray C. "The Nature, Conduct, and Acceptance," pp. 123–165.

CHAPTER 9 _____

The Use of Private Sector Management Analysts by the Federal Government

Although management analysis (MA) is often thought of as a public sector function, it occurs in the private sector as well. First, the variety of management analytical services and studies provided by "name" consulting firms is closely akin to management analysis. In a few cases, usually in small companies, the term *Management Analysis* is even used in the firm names, such as Management Analysis Company located in Atlanta and Management Analysis, Incorporated, in McLean, Virginia. The management consulting services these firms provide naturally are available to any private or public organization requesting them. This latter area, the provision of MA services to government organizations, is addressed in this chapter.

MA is a staff function that has as its main purpose the improvement of agency management policy, machinery, practices, and procedures. In today's federal environment with its emphasis on increased efficiency in agency management practices and procedures, many agencies are turning to the use of private sector management analysis support for quantitative analysis. At the same time, federal agencies tend to develop internal management studies directed toward improvement of management policy and machinery.

Quantitative analysis in support of management practices and procedures can take many forms, dictated primarily by the scope and limitations of the initial perceptions of agency management. Contracts tend to identify organizational entities to be examined, such as specific Automated Data Processing (ADP) or audiovisual entities. The private sector management analysts are therefore constrained by contract specifications from wandering too far from the basic units initially identified by the agency. This situation has advantages and disadvantages for the contracting agency. For example, if an agency contracts for a management analysis of a thirty-six-person ADP shop, the study will focus on improvements in practices and procedures within that shop, which is the intent of agency management, and will not dilute resources by considering other ADP issues within the agency. In one agency, such a study identified personnel savings of almost 50 percent, primarily through improved procedures for eliminating obsolete and redundant requirements. If, however, the requirements are obsolete or redundant because other elements of the same agency are inefficiently developing databases for personal computer operations, the personnel savings may have been made in the wrong place.

Although private firms provide the full range of management analytical services, generally, private sector management analysts are used to provide the federal government with such services as:

1. Commercial activity studies (comparing specific federal unit costs with private sector bids to provide the same services).
2. Efficiency reviews (using commercial activity study techniques to review organizations that provide services not easily delegated to private sector firms, such as personnel sections, contracting functions, and policy-making sections).
3. Work standards (determining how long it should take to perform a task).

These services are elaborated on in the following paragraphs.

The commercial activity study process became federal policy over thirty years ago and has been endorsed by every administration, Democratic and Republican, since that time. The process as practiced today encompasses the preparation of several documents. The primary document is a performance work statement (PWS), which is a precise statement of the work requirements for a specific unit or function. The PWS may delete activities currently being performed if they are deemed unnecessary, and add necessary services not currently being provided. If a contractor is subsequently selected to do the work, the PWS becomes part of his or her contract. A second document is a management study that determines the number of federal employees needed to perform the work specified in the PWS. The number of federal employees is based on quantitative data such as workload, productive hours per position, work standards, and productivity measurement.

The two documents cited above, the PWS and the management study, are also developed as part of an efficiency review. If the function is to be considered for contractor performance, that is, a full commercial activity study, then further documents are required. One is an estimate of the cost of providing the service using government employees, and a second is a technically acceptable contractor bid to provide the services called for in the PWS. The best contractor bid is then compared with the cost of government employee performance to determine how the services will be provided in the future.

A unique aspect of the full commercial activity cost comparison is the fact that the process results in a decision. If all procedures have been followed, then determination of the low bid (government employee organization compared with contractor) results in an automatic decision, not a recommendation that can be overruled. The process includes an appeals procedure to ensure that the process has been followed.

Efficiency reviews are used to assist in the streamlining of federal organizations by taking a structured look at work requirements, supervisory positions, and personnel assignments. While the principal documents are identical in format to the management study and PWS used in the commercial activity process, an efficiency review PWS has a less important role since it will never be incorporated into a contractual document. Subsequently, the emphasis in efficiency review studies is heavily oriented toward the management study. Further, since the specter of contracting out is absent from the efficiency review process, there is minimal pressure to emphasize personnel reductions as a goal.

Work standards are a powerful management tool that address many of the concerns found in the workplace. Some of these concerns are the allocation of personnel and monetary resources, equitable performance appraisals, and a general understanding between management and labor of performance goals and objectives. Work standards are essentially evaluation criteria based upon two important factors: the quality and quantity of work performed.

Developed with the appropriate emphasis on the proper component, work standards enable management to forecast the amount of work that will be performed in a given time period at a given quality level. This enables management to plan where personnel will be most effectively used. Budgets can be developed along these lines that accurately portray the future needs of the office.

These attributes themselves make work standards an appealing approach to productivity management. However, there are additional important benefits derived from standards that have an impact on worker morale. Standards provide a uniform basis against which individual performance can be measured. A common complaint from workers is that performance appraisals do not necessarily reflect an accurate picture of the volume or quality of work performed. Many times performance evaluations are influenced by personal bias rather than being primarily based on uniform criteria. The use of work standards eliminates the chances of haphazard performance appraisals since all important aspects of productivity are documented on a daily, weekly, or quarterly basis.

Goals and objectives are also defined through work standards. Employees and managers know exactly what level of productivity is expected in any given task. Short-term productivity and quality goals can be developed that help to eliminate the drudgery of overwhelming, unending tasks.

Private industry has used work standards profitably since 1760. The federal government can benefit from the use of work standards as well. In fact, emphasis was given to the need for a standards program in all governmental agencies when President Truman, by Executive Order 10072 in July 1949, and Congress, by public law, emphasized the need for the continuous examination and review of governmental operations to ensure the achievement of departmental goals and objectives.

Standards have already been successfully used in some governmental agencies. In these instances productivity levels have been raised by as much as 100 percent, saving the federal government upwards of $1 million per year.

Most federal agencies have used the services of private sector management consulting organizations to perform the specific analyses associated with the commercial activity study. The process has been formalized through Office of Management and Budget Circular Number A-76, which is a permanent directive of the executive office of the president to all executive branch agencies. The process includes identification of functions to be studied, either as commercial activity studies (competition with the private sector) or efficiency reviews (no private sector competition). This step in the process is almost always performed by internal management analysts (or individuals having a management analysis function) at a relatively high organizational level. The actual implementation of the studies and reviews is then assigned to subordinate offices that seldom have adequate staff to conduct the studies and reviews with internal resources.

A typical MA performed by private sector firms for the federal government will be defined in terms of functions to be studied and the number of government employees currently identified as performing those functions. The responsible government office prepares a statement of work and a schedule to perform the study, which are then sent to the contracting office. A formal government request for proposals (RFP) is then issued and the resultant private sector bids are evaluated. A contract is then issued to a private sector MA consulting firm.

From 1979 to 1986 the vast majority of MA consulting engagements of the nature being discussed here encompassed reviews of blue-collar work forces at federal installations. Typical examples were a transportation unit that maintained and operated government-owned vehicles or an operations unit that maintained and repaired federal buildings. Numerous reviews were conducted on the work forces at federal parks, recreation areas, and other outdoor facilities. Other functions that underwent intensive study during the same period were ADP functions (such as data entry and computer operations), audiovisual shops, and food service operations.

For commercial-activity studies and efficiency reviews, the study process to be followed by the MA team is delineated by federal guidance, but the selection of quantitative techniques is usually left to the judgment of the consulting firm. Basically, certain questions must be answered:

- What does the federal work force do?
- What should it be doing?
- How efficiently is the work being performed?
- How can the efficiency be improved?
- How many federal employees are really needed?

Typically, the consulting management analysts begin by addressing the first two questions. This step includes substantial document review since both the organization being studied and its work force are governed by statutes, agency directives, and government personnel regulations. Ideally, a job accounting system has recorded specific work assignments and labor hours by job. Frequently, however, the job accounting system has been inadequately maintained, and available data is incomplete. Regardless of the amount of historical data available, the management analysts use a variety of data collection tools to identify work being performed. These tend to include interviews, flow charting, and work sampling.

Private sector management analysts are frequently at a disadvantage in the documentation of workload data and facility and equipment information. This disadvantage is the direct outcome of the rigidity of federal contracting procedures that fail to allow for the impact of other government actions on federal record keeping. For example, federal regulations and accounting systems generally require the maintenance of equipment and real-property inventories as well as workload data. The Budget and Accounting Procedures Act of 1950 and the Administrative Procedures Act of 1949 are basic laws that have in turn been implemented by agency regulations requiring documentation. Therefore, most contracts for management analysis assume the availability and currency of data required by statute or regulation, and require the contractor to use and analyze government-furnished information applicable to the analysis. Unfortunately, when the contractor goes to the records to extract the data, it is frequently out of date or non-existent.

The reasons for the absence or obsolescence of required records, although not commendable, are fully understandable. When Congress appropriates money for the procurement of equipment or real property, the procuring agency must carefully report the expenditure of funds. Subsequently, neither the Congress nor OMB asks questions about the status of the equipment or property. Nor does OMB or Congress inquire about the accuracy of job accounting so long as the required system is in place. Within the agency there is little interest in the record-keeping mechanism if no one is going to query the records. This neglect is compounded by organizational problems. Usually, the organization responsible for record maintenance performs other functions as well. Demands for information concerning these other functions may be heavy. The natural tendency is to maintain the files that are constantly in use and to ignore the apparently dead files.

When the contractor given an MA mission arrives on the scene, he or she is prepared to go to the work order and inventory files, draw a random sample of data, and conduct an analysis. When the contractor finds that the file drawer (or automated database) is empty, he or she is in a dilemma. Without the data, the analysis fails. The contract does not call for taking inventory, and if a job order file is empty, historical data is impossible to reconstruct. Usually the contract has tight schedules that are designed to meet the needs of higher headquarters, and lower echelons in or out of government are reluctant to request waivers on existing deadlines.

Given a need to provide a product by a given date, both the government organization and the consultant are inclined to cooperate in an effort to develop a substitute methodology and to grasp at straws that might provide acceptable data. For a variety of reasons the results are frequently flawed.

From a technical point of view, the major flaw is compromise of project design. The consulting firm was probably selected because it submitted in its proposal a superior project design. The project design, in turn, should have been based on accepted industrial engineering, statistical, and management analysis practices. The substitute methodology, jointly developed in haste by the contractor's project manager and the agency's on-site manager, tends to compromise accepted practices, frequently without knowledgeable insight into the rationale for the viability of the original design. The results, particularly if the recommendations are based on assumptions concerning productivity and quality and quantity of work, may not work.

Apart from the problem areas cited above, the private sector management analyst takes a structured approach to the organizational and staffing challenges associated with a commercial activity study/efficiency review assignment. Table 9.1 displays a typical approach. The five basic questions posed earlier have been expanded into sixteen management study questions. In order to obtain answers to each question, the management analyst must interrogate many data sources. These sources may be organizational records, knowledgeable personnel both internal and external to the organization, and as the study progresses, perhaps the management analysts themselves. It is not unusual for a management analyst who is immersed in an organization for some months to become recognized as the expert on many aspects of the organization itself.

Some critical aspects of the sixteen questions tend to be unique to the federal environment. For example, a widely recognized problem in government operations is the tendency for the grade and salary of a supervisor to be directly related to the number and grades of subordinates. Therefore, many supervisors tend to look for work that can be used as a basis for increasing the number of employees under them, and frequently this additional work is tangential to the primary mission of the organizational unit. In fact, the additional work may distract from accomplishing the primary mission and have limited value to the customer. In one study conducted by the author, a federal ADP organization generated reports for users with little or no concurrence on the part of the users that the reports were helpful or necessary. As a result of the study and with internal management agreement, over half of the periodic reports that were being produced were discontinued.

An appropriate approach in responding to the first two questions on Table 9.1 is a series of interviews in which one asks supervisors and workers specifically to identify outputs of the unit. A frequently encountered situation is one in which the supervisor's list of outputs and the worker's list of outputs overlap but are not identical. In other words, the workers are doing some things that the supervisor is unaware of, and not doing some things that the supervisor believes are being accomplished. Re-interviewing is then in order to provide a unified list. This list should then be matched with statutes, regulations, and other authorization documents to ensure that higher management wants the unit to provide the identical services (no more, no less).

Oddly enough, the development of a management-approved unified list of services provided is often the most useful output of the management analysis. Government organizations have a tendency to acquire duties over the years, and to continue to provide the associated services long after the need has passed. People like to do what they are accustomed to doing, and unless directed to cease and desist, will continue to provide unwanted services. A corollary is the tendency of workers to equate service with effort rather than with utility of output.

Table 9.1
Questions, Data Sources, and Techniques

Management Study Questions	Data Sources	Management Analysis Technique
1. What does the federal work force do? (mission)	Mission Statement. Supervisors, Overhead Personnel, & Customers.	Review. Interviews.
2. What should they be doing?	Same as above, also: Statutes & Agency Regulations. Tasking Documents.	Literature Search. Review.
3. How is the federal work force organized?	Staffing Authorization. Supervisors. Current Organization Charts.	Chart. Interview. Verify.
4. How should they be organized?	Answers to 6 and 9. Organization Charts of Similar Work Forces.	Organization Analysis. Review.
5. How is the work being performed?	Employees & Supervisors. Management Analysts.	Interview. Observation and Flow

	Question	Source	Method
6.	How can the work be performed more efficiently?	Management Analysts. Employees & Supervisors. Flow Charts. Anticipated Changes in Equipment, Performance Requirements, or Resources.	Evaluate Alternatives. Solicit Recommendations. Analyze for Redundancy, Necessity, Excessive Complexity. Analyze for Effects on Work Performance.
7.	How much work is being done?	Workload Records (e.g., work orders, log books periodic reports). Employees & Supervisors.	Sample and Compile. Technical Estimating & Task Data Sheets.
8.	Which personnel do what work?	Employees & Supervisors. Position Descriptions.	Interview. Review.
9.	What type of personnel are needed to do the work?	OPM Classification Standards. Production Standards.	Review. Verify (possibly time study).

Table 9.1 (continued)

Management Study Questions	Data Sources	Management Analysis Technique
How many?	Compiled Workload Data. Engineered Performance Standards.	Staffing Analysis.
	Work Being Performed.	Short-interval Sampling.
10. How much of what materials are used?	Records of Material Usage. Supervisors & Employees.	Review. Technical Estimates.
11. What equipment belongs to the federal work force?	Equipment Inventory.	Verify with Supervisor.
12. What equipment is needed to do the work?	Equipment Inventory, Compiled Workload Data, and Recommended Staffing.	Equipment Analysis.
13. What high-tech equipment or methods are used?	Equipment Inventory. Employees & Supervisors.	Review. Interview.

14.	What high-tech methods or equipment could be used to improve efficiency or effectiveness?	Management Analysts. Technical Experts.	Observation. Consultation.
15.	What kind of facility does the work force occupy?	Facility Diagram or Layout. Facility Inventory.	Verify. Review.
16.	What facility improvements or changes would enhance the work force's efficiency or effectiveness?	Management Analysts. Technical Experts.	Observation. Consultation.

143

An employee may take great pride in the careful organization of a complex report, to include footnoting, graphics, and clear exposition. To management, however, the key question is: What do I need to know?

These problems are placed in focus by the management analyst's emphasis on dealing with outputs as the primary indicator of service performed. Once this is established, the management analyst can address effectiveness and efficiency matters. Peter Drucker once addressed efficiency and effectiveness by posing his concern with a loft full of engineers turning out beautiful blueprints for the wrong product.

Today's management analysts use quantitative tools and rigorous statements to specify the attributes of each output. These attributes include:

- A standard or standards that describe an acceptable product or service (output).
- The quantity produced (meals served, vouchers examined).
- The frequency with which the product or service is provided (units per day, week, or month).
- Labor hours involved by grade or job skill.
- Materials and/or equipment utilization incorporated into a single unit (or standard production lot).
- A valid inspection process to accept or reject delivered products or services.

The determination of the desired outputs of a unit or activity with acceptable standards, a valid inspection process, and identified resource inputs (labor, machine hours, and material) under current conditions provide a firm basis for analysis aimed at improving the efficiency and effectiveness of the organizational unit. Questions 3 and 4 in Table 9.1 now come into play. The charting of the flow of work through an organization often results in the identification of duplication of effort or bottlenecks that can be eliminated. The charting also tends to illuminate the most productive and least productive sections of the organization. This leads us to Question 5, how is the work being performed, and Question 6, how can the work be performed more efficiently.

A variety of examples observed over a thirty-year MA career seem to reoccur with great frequency. For example, the work day may be scheduled from 8:00 A.M. to 4:30 P.M. with a half-hour lunch break, but no one starts before 8:30 A.M. or performs productive work after 4:00 P.M. If a task is completed at 3:00 P.M., the workers fail to start a new task until the following day. The prime reason for these losses of productive time is the absence of a viable work assignment system, and the installation of such a system is usually a relatively simple

Figure 9.1
Alternative Blue-Collar Work Forces

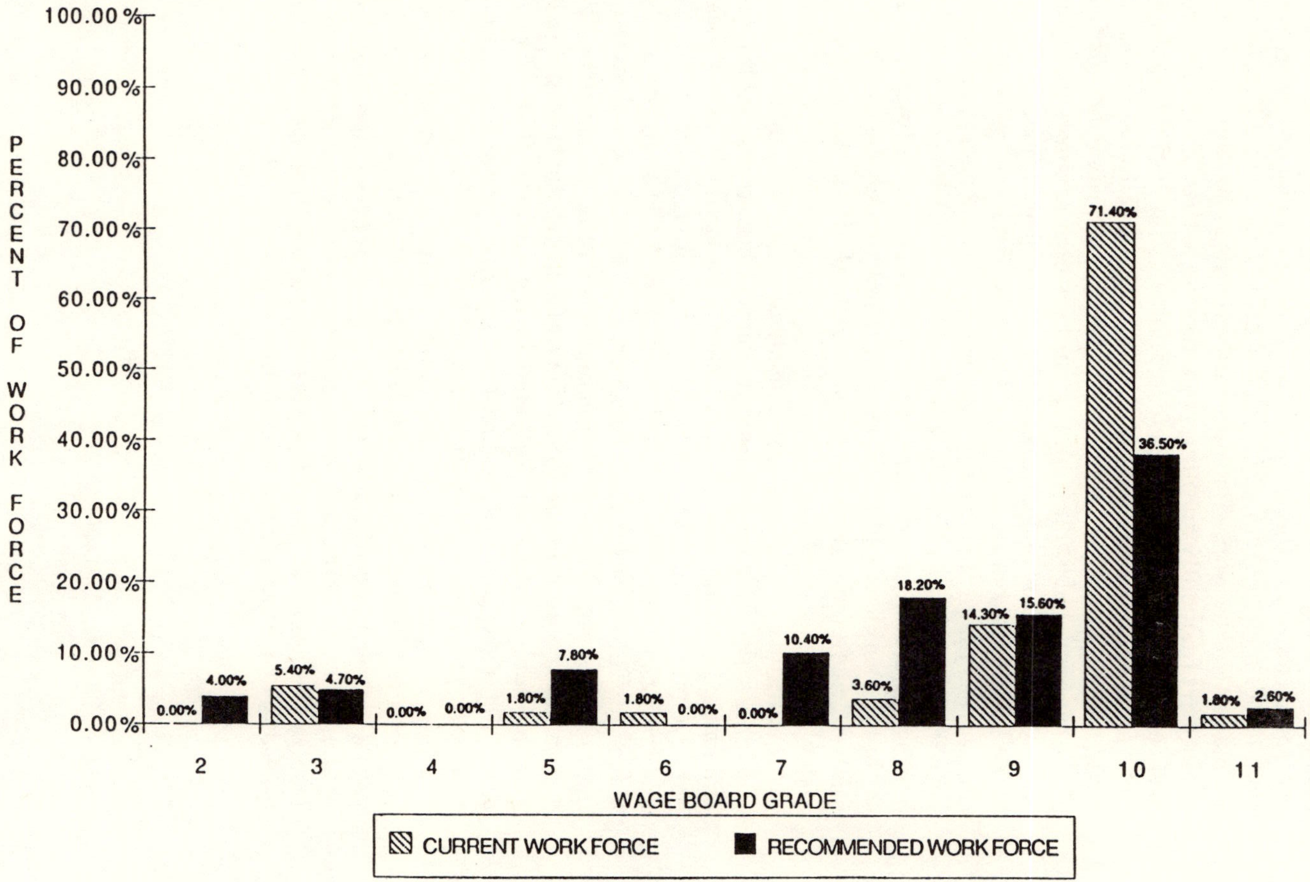

managerial process. It does, however, require that supervisors plan, rather than react to, work situations. Experience indicates that a 12.5 percent increase in efficiency is the minimum to be expected when a work assignment system is installed. This in turn means that fourteen people can do the work that previously required sixteen.

A second frequently encountered situation is that of multiple layers of supervisors. In one study of a federal blue-collar work force, the total work force of sixty-eight included twenty-seven individuals with various supervisory assignments. This layering was primarily the offshoot of the personnel classification system by which senior workers could only be rewarded by movement into the supervisory ranks. In the study being highlighted here, all of the senior supervisors, with one exception, agreed that a supervisory ratio of 1 to 7 would be an improvement over the existing ratio of 1 to 2.5. In a federal ADP organization, the best systems analyst/programmer had been promoted to branch chief so that his services could be retained. Unfortunately he continued his analyst/programmer work, and the branch, in effect, operated without a chief.

A quantitatively oriented management study will include graphic and tabular displays that show management breakouts by skill, grade, and longevity of the work force. These are particularly useful for comparative purposes and for showing the overabundance of certain skills and grades and the paucity of others. Figure 9.1 is an example of such a display. This illustration is based on a study of a navy installation's maintenance organization. The actual work force had sixty positions.

Some of the differences in the way MA is practiced in the private and the public sectors are reflected in the analysts themselves. For example, analysts in private firms are generally more specialized and tend to be more quantitatively oriented than those in the public sector. Further, the undergraduate degrees of analysts in private firms are concentrated in engineering, accounting, statistics, and the sciences, with fewer business administration and liberal arts degrees than those in the federal government. Last, although graduate degrees are common in the public sector, in private companies they are virtually required for advancement to more senior positions.

CHAPTER 10 _____

Policy Analysis and Program Evaluation: New Approaches in Management Analysis

The nature and rapidity of environmental change confronted by many organizations today means management analysis (MA) needs to go well beyond the traditional efforts concerned with improving operational efficiency. In facing their new environments, many organizations must reassess their very mission and way of doing business. These "bigger picture" problems and opportunities are both complex and ambiguous and require flexible yet powerful approaches and techniques. The paragraphs that follow dealing with policy analysis and program evaluation describe two of these approaches.

Policy analysis and program evaluation are two of the more modern and more powerful approaches in MA. They are tools for the analyst to use in assisting managers in making complex decisions and in setting policies. Usually, policy analysis is future oriented in that it is concerned with a future decision. In contrast, program evaluation is past oriented in that it is concerned with evaluating the past performance of a program or policy.

Policy analysis and program evaluation share the common perspective that government problems and issues can be addressed through quantitative means. Quantification is an approach that many researchers in public administration have selected because of their belief that it could improve understanding, predictability, and, ultimately, public decision making. Prediction in physics or chemistry, based on the interaction of nonconscious entities, is, on the whole, more accurate and reliable than are models or paradigms in public administration, which must involve the interactions of people. However, it is the author's view that an answer obtained by quantitative methods in public administration is not necessarily better than one obtained from the human relations disciplines. Often, in order to quantify a model, it might be necessary to suppress too many aspects of the problem that the model seeks to illuminate.

There were three milestones in the development and use of quantitative disciplines in public administration. First, there was the scientific management movement founded by Frederick Taylor. He views the goal of management as the achievement of the maximum prosperity for the employer combined with the maximum prosperity for the employees. Some of the elements of scientific management that can bring about this goal are time study, standardization, job training, and planning. Some of Taylor's disciples, known as "efficiency experts" or "time and motion study experts," have been criticized for taking the human element out of their paradigm. Even if there is truth in this view, at least their goal, as Taylor states, is very humanistic in tone and content.

The second milestone involved the development of operations research and related mathematical techniques during World War II. The term *operations research* is commonly used very loosely. Narrowly defined, it refers to an attempt to improve efficiency through precise mathematical algorithms. This technique has been used by public administrators for such calculations as submarine deployments and oil allocations. Broadly defined, operations research can mean most quantitative policy analysis.

The third milestone for quantitative techniques in public management and administration involved the development of Planning, Programming, and Budgeting Systems (PPBS) and cost-effectiveness analysis, introduced into the Department of Defense in 1961. PPBS, like any programming or budgeting system, is essentially a method of making choices. However, PPBS is better for determining means than ends. Thus, PPBS can tell us which weapons system to use in Europe but not whether we should be there in the first place, or how to produce a more powerful atomic bomb at less cost, but not whether to use it.

Another part of this analytical revolution at Department of Defense (DOD) was the introduction of cost-effectiveness analysis. Cost-effectiveness is a form of analysis in which the alternative actions under consideration are compared in terms of two of the consequences, dollar or resource costs, and the effectiveness associated with each alternative. The effectiveness of an alternative is measured by the extent to which that alternative, if implemented, will attain the desired objective. The preferred alternative is usually the one that produces the maximum effectiveness for a given level of cost or the minimum cost for a fixed level of effectiveness.

One possible guide for choosing between programs designed to accomplish differing objectives would be to measure the benefits and costs in the same units in all programs. In practice this means expressing both the benefits and costs in monetary units, a process that often leads to the neglect of certain benefits and costs. For example, how would a public administrator evaluate the benefit of saving lives in a hunger project? It is by attempting to reduce all outputs into one common unit of measure that cost-benefit analysis differs from cost-effectiveness analysis.

CONDUCTING A POLICY ANALYSIS

Many authors and teachers of policy analysis define it in terms of a five- or six-step process. In this author's view policy analysis can be best defined in terms of a seven-step process as follows: define the problem, define the cutting-edge issue, determine the alternatives, determine the criteria, evaluate the alternatives by the criteria, make a recommendation, and implement the chosen alternative.

Defining the problem is the first and most important step in policy analysis. It is the step where analysts tend to spend too little time and effort. Defining the problem precisely and comprehensively is vital for the rest of the analysis. If one defines the problem in too broad a fashion, then the analysis will be too general and will lose a specific focus. If one defines the problem in too narrow a fashion, then some of the most important components of the problem will be ignored.

A problem should be stated as the way conditions are now or will be in the future, the way conditions should be or could be, and the consequences of this difference. Stating a problem in this fashion defines a problem for the public agenda. This is the real power behind policy analysis—defining problems and issues for the national, state, or local agenda. When an analyst chooses to focus on minority rights, for example, as a policy analysis, that analyst is saying that this issue is important enough to command time and attention. Sometimes a policy analysis will even add an issue to the agenda of a business or government agenda.

A problem statement should typically be reworked many times during the course of a policy analysis. Usually during the third step when alternatives are considered, too numerous or too few alternatives may mean that the problem statement needs to be redefined. An analyst needs to keep an open mind about the problem statement and needs to be receptive to reworking this statement as the analysis is continued.

The second step in a policy analysis is defining a cutting-edge issue. This is the issue from which the problem depends or turns on. Two examples are in order. On the subject of abortion, the cutting-edge issue may be whether a fetus is a human life. If one feels that a fetus is a human life, then one is likely to oppose abortion; and, if one feels that a fetus is not a human life, then one is likely to support abortion on demand. Another example concerns the problem of overcrowding in jails. For this problem, the cutting-edge issue may be lack of visibility of the problem with the general public. The public is directly aware of overcrowded roads and schools, but overcrowding in jails is largely hidden from the general population. Increasing awareness of this problem is probably the first step in getting more resources allocated to solving this social problem.

Often, cutting-edge issues will involve either the visibility of the problem, such as in the overcrowding of jails, or it will involve who is responsible for solving the problem or coming up with resources to correct the problem, such as in transportation, crime, or poverty. Defining a cutting-edge issue gives the recipient of the policy analysis a new tool to use in thinking about a complex or "wicked" problem. Deciding on a cutting-edge issue is a creative process that can only occur after much research on the issue has been completed.

The third step in a policy analysis is determining the alternatives. In terms of number and type they will vary greatly depending on the specific analysis. However, some general principles do apply. For example, one should always have the status quo as a policy option. This is true for two reasons. First, the current policies may be the best choice available. Second, the status quo offers a good base case from which to measure the other alternatives. Another alternative should usually involve marginal changes from the status quo. Here, the analyst is assuming no major changes in the program or in the structure of providing benefits, but, instead, only a slight change in resource allocation or slight changes in policies or procedures. Finally, one alternative should represent fairly radical change where the analyst uses creativity to expand out of the bounds of the current system to consider new ways of doing business.

One major issue concerning alternatives is whether politically unfeasible alternatives should be included in the analysis. In this author's view they should be included because what is unfeasible today might become realistic tomorrow. Also, the analyst may wish to let the client make the final decision about political feasibility. A better option is to include politically unfeasible alternatives in the analysis but not to recommend them for implementation.

The fourth step in a policy analysis is the determination of the criteria to be applied. Authors and teachers of policy analysis list many criteria that can be used. However, in this author's judgment there are four primary criteria that should always be considered. The first criterion is efficiency. This can be defined as output divided by input.

The second criterion is effectiveness. Here the issue involves meeting established goals. Too often in public administration and in policy analysis efficiency is given more importance than is effectiveness. Perhaps this is because it is easier to measure and because many public institutions do not have clear goals from which to measure effectiveness. The third criterion is political feasibility, which involves a political judgment.The final criterion is equity, the most difficult criteria to measure and define. However, in any policy change there are always winners and losers. One key in equity is to examine who are these winners and losers. Another key is to examine who pays for the benefits being considered and who will receive these benefits.

The fifth step in a policy analysis is to evaluate the alternatives by the criteria. This is really the heart of policy analysis. Some analysts develop a matrix where each alternative is presented in rows and each criterion in columns, and the intersections are rank ordered or given different weights. One option is to develop elaborate statistical models to evaluate the alternatives. Another is simply to discuss each alternative in relation to criteria in a narrative form. The real purpose is to lay out clearly the pros and cons of each alternative and consider these in a logical and intelligent manner.

The sixth step is to select a preferred alternative and make a recommendation. If the fifth step is completed properly, this step is a natural outcome. Sometimes more than one alternative seem attractive and this is proper to point out. However, whatever the recommendation, a good policy analysis allows the client or recipient to pick another alternative from that selected by the analyst.

The last step is one frequently excluded from many policy analysis texts: implementing the chosen alternative or policy. However, it is important to emphasize that writing a policy analysis in itself changes nothing. It is only through effective implementation that we make a difference. Sometimes this step is ignored because it is considered to be in the framework of program evaluation and not policy analysis. However, if this step is to be considered the important final stage in a policy analysis, it will need some coverage and consideration. The primary issue here is how best to monitor effective program implementation. This author feels that comprehensive policy analyses should address this important subject.

ISSUES IN POLICY ANALYSIS

Five key questions or issues that relate to policy analysis are:

1. What factors contribute to and limit the use of policy analysis in government?

2. Can policy analysis be value-free?

3. How does politics affect policy analysis?

4. What general models or frameworks are available for policy analysis?

5. What is the state of policy analysis in government at the current time?

Some of the factors that affect policy analysis in government include:

1. *Short and simple analysis.* The primary problem with most policy analysis in government has been that analysis is often long and complicated. Analysis that is short and simple for nontechnical people to read and understand is most effective and has the best chance of successfully moving up the chain of command.

2. *Analysis that is perceived as supporting senior positions.* Analysis that supports "the party line" or the previous positions of senior career or political officials is most likely to be used. This is not to say that analysis is not sometimes effective in changing views and opinions, but this is the exception, not the general rule.

3. *Access to data and to the decision makers.* Good access to data and information, library resources for example, can greatly aid in the development of relevant and useful analysis. Also, the availability of senior decision makers is crucial so that through the course of the analysis the analyst can ask questions as issues come up. Some government executives establish a group of management analysts to work directly for them. In such an operation there is usually good interaction between analysts and decision makers. However, where analytical functions are located far from the decision makers, either geographically or organizationally, then the reverse situation is likely to occur.

4. *Timeliness of analysis.* If a decision maker requests that a policy analysis be performed, it is usually because an issue is "hot," and more information or ideas would be useful. However, in the federal government, issues tend to be hot for limited periods of time, and the ability of a management analyst to be aware of and respond to this important time window is crucial if the analysis is to be relevant and useful.

5. *Resources.* In the federal government there are large analytical shops and there are single analysts by themselves in operational offices. Obviously, an analyst is limited by resources and should keep these limitations in mind when attempting to establish realistic expectations from decision makers.

6. *Knowledge and ability of the analyst.* An analyst is limited by knowledge and ability. Knowledge is affected by an analyst's background and by time available for study and ability to learn. The ability of analysts does vary in all organizations, but ability is primarily related to the capability to model a problem simply and accurately and write it up concisely.

7. *Political feasibility of intervention.* Often an analyst recommends that some action be taken or that resources be channeled toward a particular problem.

Here the analyst must be clear that what is being recommended is politically and economically feasible or else previous efforts will have little impact.

8. *Systems are open and uncertain.* Most human systems are subject to many variables external to the system and subject to great uncertainty. This makes human systems difficult to model and explain. The analyst must decide how to define and limit the analysis so that it is both useful and manageable.

The second issue to be explored is whether policy analysis can ever be value-free. The answer to this question is a resounding "No"! In fact, a rigorous attempt to make policy analysis value-free has the consequence of hiding bias and assumptions, not eliminating them. It is perhaps better to bring biases out in the open where they can be observed and evaluated. "The New Public Administration" is, in fact, a rejection of value-free public administration. Under this concept, analysts and administrators should be advocates for social change and improvement. This view is in contrast to the classical notion of pure, value-free analysis.

Even scientific observations may not be totally neutral or value-free. Phenomenology, as a discipline of public administration, tries to explain the social world as a construct of human consciousness. This idea may appear a little extreme to some, but it is not difficult to imagine how bias can affect our judgments and our analyses.

In fact, in a well-performed policy analysis there are two areas in which values should be explicitly stated and discussed. First, it is important to state how the various "stakeholders" view alternative decisions or actions. Second, the fundamental values of the analyst that may affect the analysis can and should be listed as assumptions.

There are two general points that are important to understand about value-free analysis. The first point is that the illusion of objectivity gives policy analysis a certain type of credibility in the bureaucracy. A decision maker will sometimes turn to analysis in an argument to demonstrate that his or her decisions are motivated primarily by facts and not by personal bias. The second point is that the selection of a particular problem or issue to analyze is, in itself, a decision based on values. For example, poverty has existed as long as has mankind, but why did national attention and much analysis begin to focus on this area only in the 1960s and not before? Sometimes a culture has to be ripe for such analysis. The main point here is that when a decision maker asks for a policy analysis on poverty, he or she is implicitly stating that someone cares about poverty and that the government is considering reacting to the problem in a new and different way.

A third issue is the effect of politics on policy analysis. Unfortunately for those with an idealistic view of policy analysis, much government analysis is committed to legitimizing policies, not analyzing or establishing them. For example, DOD is turning out much analysis in support of Strategic Defense Initiative (SDI), a system whose deployment has been approved by the current and past administrations.

There are at least five characteristics that help determine whether analysis is legitimacy-oriented or policy choice-oriented.

1. *Time horizon.* Short time horizons tend to produce an advocacy environment because there is insufficient time to examine alternatives, criteria, and policy trade-offs.

2. *Survival orientation.* Analyses that have policy implications directly affecting the survival of the policy maker are not usually allowed to be impartial or neutral. Advocacy is a natural outcome when self-interest is involved in a policy debate.

3. *Level of social concern.* Issues that arouse significant public concern and that involve strong interest-group pressures will tend to move toward advocacy analysis, while with more neutral issues having minimal social impacts, alternatives, criteria, and assumptions can be considered without pressure.

4. *Technical versus social issues.* Technical problems with physical parameters are more susceptible to policy-choice analysis than is the case for social issues that have strong value and ethical components. It is true that ethical trade-offs can be considered in policy analysis, but they are difficult to scope and to quantify or measure.

5. *Complexity.* Simple problems with manageable boundaries are more susceptible to policy-choice analysis than are more-complex issues of great magnitude.

The main problem in the link between politics and analysis involves the short-run orientation of politics. In politics, success is measured in terms of results delivered in months or, at best, over two to three years. Many social problems require investments that will not see returns for five, ten, or even twenty years. The weight of politics in government, at least at the highest levels, means that there is a very high discount rate on benefits. Managers often need results now, not five or ten years from now. This political orientation means that good alternatives may not be considered, or that if considered, they may be restricted.

A fourth issue is that of the models or frameworks available for policy analysis. David E. Wilson outlines five basic models or approaches including the rational approach, the incremental approach, the mixed-scanning approach, the general systems approach, and the learning-adaptive approach.[1]

The rational approach is probably the best-known model of decision making and the one most used in policy analysis. The rational approach can be defined as the scientific method as applied to the social sciences. The rational approach is a comprehensive explanation of goals, conditions, alternative strategies, costs and benefits of alternatives, probabilities of events, and optimal solutions. Herbert Simon limited rationality through the concept of "Grounded Rationality" and that of "satisfying" versus maximization. Criticisms of the rational approach usually center around the informational demands placed on the analyst and the claim that "wicked problems" in the social sciences are usually concerned with value problems rather than factual issues.

The incremental approach is the major alternative to the rational approach in policy analysis. Charles Lindblom first suggested a concept of "disjointed incrementalism," a refinement of "muddling through" which he had formulated earlier.[2] Incrementalism can be summarized as several items including the following:

• Policy analysts should focus on incremental change rather than major change.
• Policy analysts should consider only a restricted number and variety of policy alternatives and policy consequences.
• Ends should be adjusted in terms of feasible means.
• Analysis is not centralized, but is socially fragmented.

Thus incrementalism tends to reflect the realities and constraints of the workplace while still offering analysis as something of value for decision making. Criticisms of this approach or model include the following claims:

• It is too conservative and noninnovative.
• It does not apply in an environment of rapid changes where new directions and ideas are needed.
• It may be risky to ignore some alternatives of consequences.

One could argue that the rational approach is normative, a model to strive for in policy analysis, and the incremental approach is descriptive of the realities of policy analysis in the government.

The mixed-scanning approach was developed by Amitai Etzioni.[3] This method attempts to combine the best features of the other approaches into a synthetic approach. It is not clear from Etzioni's discussion how the flexibility of this approach would operate in practice. However, under the basic approach, strategic scanning and goal-setting would operate simultaneously with lower-level, short-run probing and scanning.

The general systems approach seeks reorientation of thought using the model of a system as a paradigm. Systems theory tends to focus on the mathematical relation between parts of a system and the relation of a system to its environment. There are two kinds of systems: open systems, analogous to biological organisms that react to their environment; and closed systems, analogous to physics, which involves internal laws and operations. Criticism of this approach includes the claim that it is too mechanistic and too demanding of knowledge.

Finally, the learning-adaptive model is the newest—and in some ways the most interesting—of the approaches. This approach stems from the culture of the 1960s in terms of dealing with turbulent environments and failure of the rational approach to improve human conditions. Some principles of this approach include the following:

- Organizations are made up of communication networks.
- Organizational change is a complex learning process seeking changed states of behavior.
- Face-to-face relations between expert and client are essential.
- Healthy organizations can change and adapt to their environments.
- Emphasis should be placed on nonbureaucratic structures and processes.

This approach involves a continuous cycle of feedback and evolution in which man's psychosocial development is a central focus of planning. Criticisms of this approach include the difficulty in reaching consensus solutions to social problems and the limits of psychology and sociology in analytical policy analysis.

The final issue is the general state of policy analysis in government today. The single most important factor in assessing the state of policy analysis is the possibility that most of the easy problems in government have been satisfactorily dealt with and that only the "wicked" problems remain. This is comparable to debt collection when you try to collect the easy debts first, while the difficult ones remain uncollected. Problems are "wicked" in the sense that they defy efforts to define their boundaries and to identify their causes and solutions.

PROGRAM EVALUATION

The last area to be explored in this chapter is program evaluation. In contrast to policy analysis, program evaluation addresses a current or past program or decision. Usually the question to be asked is whether a program was truly effective in meeting its goals. One type of program evaluation that has considerable merit and has received much attention is called an "evaluability assessment" (EA). Joseph S. Wholey developed this concept in some detail.[4] Wholey describes the goals of an EA as the enhanced ability to answer three questions:

1. Is the program ready to be managed for results?
2. What changes are needed to allow results-oriented management?
3. Is evaluation likely to contribute to improved program performance?

In this regard EAs help managers overcome five potential problems:

1. Lack of agreement on program objectives and information priorities.
2. Implausibility of program objectives.
3. Unavailability of relevant information on program performance.
4. Management inability or unwillingness to act on the basis of program performance information.
5. Management inability to communicate the value of program activities.

As for process, Wholey says the initial focus on EAs is on program intent. Here the evaluator documents program objectives, expectations, causal assumptions, information needs, priorities of relevant managers, policy makers, and interest groups, and clarification of the performance indicators.

In the Wholey framework, evaluators use three sources of information: program documentation, interviews with program managers and policy makers, and interviews with representatives of relevant interest groups. On the basis of information from these sources, the evaluators develop two sets of products. These products (program design models and lists of currently agreed-upon program performance indicators) document the extent of agreement on program objectives and document the types of information that could be developed in terms of performance indicators.

Program design models present the program design, which includes the resources allocated to the program, intended program activities, expected program outcomes, and assumed linkages. Also, in most programs, management has a system for monitoring program activities but has not clearly defined the intended outcomes and intended impacts of program activities. These types of agreed-upon performance indicators are crucial for focusing top-level attention on possible problem areas in which goals are not being met (exception reporting).

In the Wholey system the second focus of evaluability assessments is on program reality. Here the evaluator documents the feasibility of measuring program performance and estimates the likelihood that program objectives will be achieved. Using existing documentation and site visits to a small number of projects, the evaluators determine the extent to which intended resources, activities, and outcomes are likely to materialize. At this point three intermediate products can be developed: models of resource flows, process flows, and information flows.

To assist in making decisions on the set of objectives in terms of which a program is to be managed and held accountable, Wholey includes an analysis of the plausibility of program objectives. On the basis of what has been learned from program documentation, from interviews with program managers, policy makers, and representatives of relevant interest groups, and from site visits, the evaluators estimate the chances that each objective will be achieved at an acceptable level. Wholey explains that these plausibility analyses have changed evaluability assessment from a pre-evaluation process to an evaluation process. Thus, the plausibility analysis represents the evaluator's judgments on the likely success of the program.

The third focus is on management use of evaluability assessment information to improve program design, program performance, and use of program performance information. Using the information gathered and analyzed in the first two evaluability assessment steps, the evaluators are now in a position to work with management by exploring options for program change and program improvement.

The evaluable model of the program presents, in summary form, an evaluation of the program design. The evaluable program is that portion of the program that is currently manageable in relation to a set of realistic program objectives and agreed-upon program performance indicators. Being able to identify what portion of the program is now evaluable and what steps need to be taken to increase this proportion is one of the key outputs of any EA.

Approaches such as policy analysis and program evaluation are needed today, given the complexity, breadth, and ambiguity of problems faced by many organizations. The concepts, techniques, and tools associated with them are sufficiently developed to be useful to the practicing analyst. The management analyst who understands and can apply these approaches will find his services in demand, particularly by top level officials who must wrestle with the most fundamental issues in their organizations.

NOTES

1. David Wilson, *The National Planning Idea in U.S. Public Policy: Five Alternative Approaches* (Boulder, Colo.: Western Press, 1980).

2. David Braybrooke and Charles Lindblom, *A Strategy of Decision: Policy Evaluation as a Social Process* (New York: The Free Press, 1963).

3. Amitai Etzioni, *The Active Society* (New York: The Free Press, 1971).

4. Joseph Wholey, *Evolution and Effective Public Management* (Boston: Little, Brown, and Co., 1983).

CHAPTER II _____

New Developments in Public Administration and Their Implications for Management Analysis

This chapter will focus on new developments in public administration and their implications for management analysis over the 1965 to 1990 time frame. What happens in public administration is important to MA for a number of reasons. First, a significant number of management analysts are employed in the public sector. In addition, a good number of graduates of public administration programs work in federal, state, and local government. Further, many practicing management analysts have degrees in public administration. Last, trends and initiatives in government administration, such as the contracting out of government functions under Office of Management and Budget Circular A-76 and federal policy on information management provided by the Paperwork Reduction Act of 1980 and Office of Management and Budget Circular A-130, affect the nature of management analytical services provided by the private sector.

The theme of the chapter is that the issues, events, theories, and practice of public administration and their implications for MA can be best understood and analyzed within the framework of certain unifying themes. Some of these themes are not unique to the period 1965–1990; however, all of them assume special relevancy over the recent past. These basic unifying themes include: (1) "The New Public Administration," (2) decentralization, (3) administration and politics, (4) participation, (5) efficiency and productivity, (6) public administration tools, (7) cutback management, (8) postindustrial growth, (9) stability and change, (10) public administration as a profession, (11) the public choice model, (12) Japanese management, and (13) quality.

The late 1960s was a period of many cross currents in the United

States. On the one hand, we had just passed through a decade of relative economic prosperity, and the moon landing gave us a sense of confidence. On the other hand, the tragedy of Vietnam and racial riots drained our strength. It was with this background that two key events occurred in public administration in the late 1960s. First was "the crisis of identity" for public administration. In late 1967 Waldo stated:

Both the nature and boundaries of the subject matter and the methods of studying and teaching this subject matter became problematical. Now, two decades after the critical attacks, the crisis of identity has not been resolved satisfactorily. Most of the important theoretical problems of public administration relate to this continuing crisis, to ways in which it can be resolved and to the implications and results of possible resolutions.[1]

The second event that had major ramifications for public administration was The Minnowbrook Conference and the emergence of "The New Public Administration." H. George Frederickson in *New Public Administration* gives an excellent account of this innovative period.[2] In late 1967 most of the leading theorists were invited to a conference sponsored by the American Academy of Political Science. The chair of the conference, James C. Charlesworth, summarized the purpose of this conference:

To make a bold and synoptic approach to the discipline of public administration and ... to measure the importance of public administration in the broad philosophic context.[3]

At the conclusion of the conference a final report was produced which contained a number of significant conclusions: (1) the political/administrative dichotomy is unnecessary, (2) it is not proper to mark sharply the boundaries of public administration, (3) the theory or theories of public administration are in disarray, (4) administrative or managerial issues are being replaced by political or policy issues, (5) professional schools for public administration should be encouraged, and (6) public administration should address itself to the pressing social issues of the day.[4]

There were two types of criticism of this conference.[5] First, many of the younger participants thought that the conference had avoided the major controversial issues of the time, including Vietnam and race riots. Second, Waldo was critical of the absence of the public administrators and professors of the next generation. He noted that the conferees were generally in their fifties and sixties. From this deficiency was born the idea of a separate conference dealing with public administration and limited to people thirty-five or younger. Thus the Minnowbrook Conference took place, and most authors consider this event the initial formulation of the premises and axioms of the "new public administration." Frank Marini identified the major themes at the Minnowbrook Conference as relevance, postpositivism, adaptation to a turbulent environment, and new forms of organization.[6]

The "new public administration" was not new; however, it did represent a response to changing conditions and events and a different focus or a change of priorities, a sign of growth and health in any field or profession. The basic core of traditional public administration might be described as the pursuit of Simon's concept of efficiency together with a dynamic and changing balance among Kaufman's three basic values: representativeness, politically neutral competence, and executive leadership.[7] In support of the view that the new public administration is not really new, Frederickson describes it as a search for new modes of representativeness. "We are simply entering a period during which political responsiveness is to be purchased at a cost in administrative efficiency."[8]

The new public administration emphasizes several fundamental values. First is the emphasis on social equity. The notion of social equity has several dimensions:

Social equity emphasizes equality in government services. Social equity emphasizes responsibility for decisions and program implementation for public managers. Social equity emphasizes change in public management. Social equity emphasizes responsiveness to the needs of public organizations. Social equity emphasizes an approach to the study of and education for public administration that is interdisciplinary, applied, problem solving in character, and sound theoretically.[9]

Second is the rejection of value-free public administration. Since it is clear to the new public administration that administrators both execute and make policy, it follows that they must have a sense of ethics and commitment in order to know what policies to advocate. If administrators are not neutral, then they must be committed to both efficiency and social equity.

Finally, the new public administration is committed to change. "Simply put, new public administration seeks to change those policies and structures that systematically inhibit social equity."[10] Traditional bureaucracy values stability. The new public administration, in its search for change, is willing to experiment with different organizational forms including increased decentralization.

This lack of neutrality has major implications for MA. In the classical sense, MA is considered to be an objective presentation of the pros and cons of a past program or future decision. However, as public administration is prepared to move towards a political orientation, with change and commitment as important components, the nature of MA may change with it. Over the past fifteen years MA has become oriented toward justifying policies and positions rather than making decisions about policies and positions. This political orientation of MA seems to be on the increase and has potentially serious implications.

A second key theme over the past fifteen years involves the increased popularity of decentralization. Decentralization has become a popular theme, almost a panacea, in terms of returning government to the people and increasing their participation in it. However, the federal government still appears to be attracted to centralization as an approach to new or major problems. For example, the popular notion of creating a drug czar at the federal level is indicative of this type of thinking.

MA is relevant in either a centralized or a decentralized environment. In a centralized environment, MA is often concentrated closer to the most senior decision makers. A good example here is the Office of System Analysis in the Department of Defense in the early 1960s. In a decentralized environment, such as that of the Department of Defense today, MA tends to be more diversified and geographically spread out.

The third unifying theme involves the contrast between administration and politics. Kaufman points out that the pattern is cyclical, and that the current pattern of allowing more politics into administration will eventually be replaced by the inverse trend.[11] Waldo explains that discarding the political/administrative dichotomy has not been an easy or simple step: "What should give us pause and induce humility is that a generation after the discrediting of 'politics-administration' we have made little progress in developing a formula to replace it."[12] There are definite risks in allowing administrators or unelected officials to make policy and set priorities because, unlike in the political arena, there are few explicit checks and balances in bureaucracies.

Perhaps a possible compromise lies with what Waldo terms "a new world view or a new sensibility" in the current generation of young people joining public service and universities,[13] who might be a generation of administrators not oriented toward setting policy but who have certain ethical and social values that will bound the set of permissible policies and will demand some caring and commitment. Hence, the effect on MA could be seen not as a "politicization" of analysis as much as analysis with more heart.

A fourth key theme involves the notion of participation. Waldo defines this concept in terms of two dimensions:

Participation can mean and will be used here to mean "centrifugal" forces both within and upon an organization. It means that the rank and file in an organization individually and/or collectively should have more authority and autonomy in making decisions and taking actions regarding (1) the rights and privileges of the rank and file within the organization, or (2) organizational purposes, or (3) both. It also means that those formally outside the organization, the "clientele" or affected persons, should be permitted to participate in some measure in defining goals and carrying out programs.[14]

Within the framework of the concept of participation, one hope and one fear exist. The hope is that the orientation of the new public administration and the emphasis on decentralization may help return a sense of relevance and commitment that has not been in full flower since the early 1960s. Perhaps we can learn from the Greeks and their concept of the *polis* in which several thousand people participated actively in self-government. Today, most eligible voters still choose not to get involved in the most basic democratic right. However, the greatest danger comes from the feeling of individual helplessness that has been so widespread over the recent past. This is, perhaps, the greatest challenge confronting public administrators—maintaining the perception that an individual can make a difference in a society of increasing complexity, size, and time compression. If individuals cannot make a difference, can MA do so? If individuals believe that their actions, including analysis, are irrelevant, then their belief might prove to be a self-fulfilling prophecy.

A fifth unifying theme is a basic one for public administration—efficiency. Although this is one of the classic goals of public administration, much recent writing, especially of those seeking the new public administration, often evidences a hostility toward efficiency and productivity. The significance of this hostility is that efficiency has been visualized as a mortal enemy of social justice. There are two important points concerning this debate. First, no single scholar, not even Simon, advocates efficiency as the only goal or measure of success for public administration. For example, dictatorships have been labeled as more efficient than democracies are in decision-making processes; however, few public administrators would advocate this form of government for the United States. This is because efficiency is only one criterion in MA among many others, including effectiveness, equity, and political feasibility, which must be balanced and preserved. However, MA is grounded in efficiency and can trace its roots to Taylor and scientific management where efficiency is emphasized. Second, a reasonable question to be posed to those who oppose efficiency is what is the alternative, inefficiency? Perhaps over the past twenty-five years there has been a realization that producing the maximum output for a given level of input is worthwhile only within the higher context of pursuing reasonable and acceptable social goals. To achieve efficiency in a program that is not effective or that is not morally sound may not be a goal worth achieving.

However, Waldo points out that efficiency is a unifying concept and goal in public administration and is not likely to leave the scene:

But a world without the concepts of efficiency and economy would indeed differ profoundly from the one we know. Perhaps it need not resemble that of pre-scientific and preindustrial man. But it is not clearly foreshadowed in any contemporary society whose image we could use for comparison and emulation.[15]

It is ironic that as efficiency has come under attack from some circles, the very tools that make the pursuit for efficiency more realistic and viable have also come into their own in public administration. The most visible and controversial of these tools include planning, programming, and budgeting systems (PPBS), cost-benefit analysis, and zero-base budgeting (ZBB).

Frederickson raises the interesting question of whether these tools are really objective and neutral or whether they have served advocacy purposes:

Other organizational tools such as programming-planning-budgeting systems, policy analysis, productivity measurement, zero-base budgeting, and reorganization, can be seen as enhancing change in the direction of social equity. They are almost always presented in terms of good management as a basic strategy, because it is unwise to advocate change frontally. In point of fact, however, these tools can be used as basic devices for change.[16]

This issue leads directly into the important theme of stability and change in public administration. One of the key questions and unresolved issues in public administration is how to walk the tightrope between bureaucratic stability and the changes required by dynamic involvement and increasing expectations.

MA can be used as a tool to justify the status quo or as a tool for change. Few would argue that bureaucracy is essentially conservative and that this stability represents a much-needed force in our democracy. Waldo states:

Bureaucracy, especially governmental bureaucracy, is to a society what a flywheel is to a machine or ballast to a sailing ship. Its indispensable function is to provide the element of predictability, stability, and continuity which, if missing, would result in imbalance and might lead to chaos or catastrophe.[17]

However, this concept of bureaucracy and bureaucratic decision making seems to run counter to the time compression in the modern world. If decisions must be made early and quickly in a complex and changing environment, will our current organizational incentives and structures allow this to happen? There are two points worth making about this question. First, if our institutions cannot cope with this difficult dilemma, then frustrations could lead to a dangerous overcentralization. Second, there is some hope in experimenting with alternative forms of organization to cope with time compression. Perhaps a combination of decentralizing certain functions such as education, police, road construction, and welfare, and increasing centralization on others such as planning, research and development, and international trade could be one interesting option.

Another key theme over the 1970s and 1980s with special relevance in the current political arena is "cutback management." During the 1960s, the key management problem for both business and government was how to manage growth and expansion. John Kenneth Galbraith called this a "problem of affluence." However, with the coming of limited economic growth and fiscal austerity, best evidenced by the Gramm-Rudman Act, the primary issue has shifted to management of scarcity and cutback management. Greenhalgh and McKersie make the point that public managers still do not fully understand the costly side effects of large layoffs.[18] Perhaps this is because it is a relatively new phenomenon for the current generation of managers. Although it is intrinsically less exciting to plan how to dismantle the Office of Education than it is to meet the challenge of landing a man on the moon, it is also true that expansions, but especially cutbacks, demand the most competent and humane management feasible. This author would not be surprised to see the term *cutback management* eliminated from the public administrators' vocabulary as it becomes a standard part of any public manager's repertoire.

MA can play an important role in either expansions or cutbacks, but perhaps it is even more vital in a cutback role. This is a far more difficult task than is deciding how to allocate additional resources. For this mission, MA may assume a new importance over the next decade if it can aid decision makers who must cope with increasingly difficult choices.

Another trend over the past decade has been the continuation and acceleration of what has been called postindustrial growth. Waldo points to seven characteristics of this movement from industrialism to postindustrialism: First is the emergence of knowledge as a crucial factor in productivity. Second is the emergence of information technology. The growth of the computer industry has been one of the landmark events of the past twenty-five years. Third is the decline of the factory. Automation of complete production processes is now occurring. Fourth is the emergence of new power centers. If information is power, then the people who manage our information are becoming increasingly powerful as automation increases efficiency. This can have a major implication for MA, which has the capability of both generating and refining information. Fifth is the reemphasis from production to distribution. Sixth is the shift from production to service occupations. Some economists point out that this trend is primarily responsible for our declining productivity. The final characteristic is the speeding up of change, already discussed.[19]

Another relevant theme in public administration is the movement toward a profession. Four criteria can be used to determine whether public administration is a true profession: formalized training programs in a skill, a formalized organization to bring the profession together, a concept of service orientation, and the notion of cultural tradition with a sense of identity and history. In 1965, public administration could not have met these demanding criteria, but by 1990, public administration had become a serious candidate for being a true profession. In recent years we have witnessed a late stage of professional development for public administration in accordance with the model of Harold Wilensky:

The process of professionalization begins with the emergence of a full-time occupation which develops a self-conscious concern for the development of schools for training of practitioners. These schools of training, at first organized outside of the universities, gravitate toward association with them. Professional organizations then emerge, followed by a struggle over defining the central tasks of the practice between the old guard, who were trained largely through raw experience, and the new practitioners, who emerge in increasing numbers from the professional schools. Next, the emergent profession struggles with neighboring occupations over the boundaries of professional activity; a drive for licensing and legal recognition proves successful; and finally, codes of ethics and mechanisms for their enforcement appear.[20]

A related question is whether MA qualifies as a profession. There are formalized education and training programs for MA; there are a variety of magazines and professional organizations oriented to analysis; there is an emerging consensus that analysis must be coupled with commitment; there is a cultural tradition of analysis in industry and government that is new but developing. The basic problem preventing MA from becoming a full-fledged profession is the same problem that exists in public administration: the lack of an integrating theory to connect the separate types of analysis into one overall framework or school of thought. The term *management science* is perhaps the most integrating term in MA.

Frederickson points to five major models in public administration: the classic bureaucratic model of Weber, Wilson, and Taylor, the neo-bureaucratic model of Simon and March, the institutional model of Lindblom and Mosher, the human relations model of McGregor and Likert, and the public choice model of Ostrom, Buchanan, and Mitchell.[21] Although there is no single theory of public administration, the public choice model may be the closest thing we have to a unifying theory in the field today; this theory represents one of the most exciting intellectual developments over the past twenty-five years, and this theory still offers the potential student or researcher an immense array of fertile territory for further model development and synthesis.

Vincent and Elinor Ostrom's excellent article on public choice theory points to two underlying premises of public choice theory:

Public choice represents another facet of work in political economy with more radical implications for the theory of public administration. Most political economists in the public choice tradition begin with the individual as the basic unit of analysis. Traditional economic man is replaced by "man: the decision maker." The second concern in the public choice tradition is with the conceptualization of public goods as the type of event associated with the output of public agencies.[22]

The authors point to *four basic assumptions* about individual behavior in public choice theory: individuals are assumed to be self-interested, individuals are assumed to be rational, individuals are assumed to adopt maximizing strategies, and an explicit assumption needs to be made concerning individuals' levels of information.

There are two features that are especially attractive about public choice theory in public administration. First, it offers some possibilities for government to develop different incentives or funding mechanisms that often incorporate the notion of government acting more like a business. Some such mechanisms include user taxes, service charges, and voucher systems. Second, public choice theory offers fertile territory for theory expansion. Starting with the objective function of the maximization of the social good, public choice theory offers to the potential management analyst significant opportunities to make meaningful contributions. Frederickson explains:

The modern version of political economies is now customarily referred to as either "nonmarket economics" or the "Public Choice" approach. This body of knowledge is rich in tradition and intellectual rigor, but somewhat light in empirical evidence. Nevertheless, the public choice theorists are having and will continue to have an important influence on American public administration.[23]

Another area of potential interest is Japanese management techniques. With the emergence of Japan as a major economic power and competitor with the United States, an important question is how Japan accomplished this significant achievement. Is there anything that we can learn from their experience? Here the management analyst has a difficult but important role to play because what works in one culture might not work well in another. Pascale and Athens in their excellent book, *The Art of Japanese Management,* explain:

We do not encourage direct copying of their techniques, or even their management and cultural philosophy. Their techniques, taken piecemeal, all too often wither in our climate; we cannot assume their philosophies whole even if we want to, which most of us don't. We want to look at the Japanese as if they were a special kind of mirror, one which might allow us to see ourselves in some new ways that may suggest directions for careful change.[24]

These and other authors have used MA to attempt to understand some of the secrets of the Japanese success. Some of the elements of the Japanese management style that may have some value in the United States include:

• more emphasis on education and training
• more investment and R&D
• lifetime career development
• use of consensus and collaboration
• strong view of loyalty and interdependence.

Perhaps the greatest single difference between U.S. and Japanese management is the fact that the Japanese have a long-range view of their people and enterprises, and thus are willing to spend more to develop, train, and educate their workforce and improve their systems. The U.S. view is more oriented toward short-term profitability, and in the case of the federal government, toward short-term political gains. This lack of mobility to plan and think in the long term is perhaps our single greatest weakness. MA can show that good investments now will reap big returns later; however, unless our orientation is long term, this type of analysis will stay on the shelf.

The last unifying theme involves quality. The notion of quality has several different meanings, including the quality of life, product quality, and quality control. Since the majority of the U.S. population has achieved a standard of living where the basic necessities of life are almost taken for granted, a key area of focus becomes the quality of life. Since the quality of life is harder to define and measure than are subsistence-related items, this new focus represents a challenge for

MA. If a key role of government is to improve the quality of life of its citizens, then MA must meet this challenge of definition and measurement. Also, quality involves product quality and quality control. Industrial management and public administration have been criticized, especially in the 1970s and 1980s, for delivering goods and services that lacked quality. By 1980 the U.S. automobile had become almost a symbol of the lack of attention to quality and quality control in U.S. industries. Again, quantitative factors are easier to measure than is quality. The key for U.S. management here is to incorporate a commitment to quality equal to that which already exists for time and costs. The task for MA is to include quality considerations in policy analysis and program evaluation so that quality considerations help in making final decisions.

Looking to the future of public administration and MA, it is worth asking what ideas or lessons of the past are important to carry forward. There are two thoughts in this regard. The first concerns the "crisis of public administration." If this crisis is primarily concerned with the lack of a single theory or paradigm or even a single direction of inquiry for public administration, then it will likely carry into the decade of the 1990s. However, this crisis can be viewed as a sign of health in a field or profession still able to accept new ideas and still undergoing transformation.

Another issue for the 1990s will be how to couple the relatively new fiscal and expenditure austerity with the need for social equity. If history is a valid guide, those at the lower end of the economic spectrum usually bear a disproportionate share of any cutbacks. Can MA find more-creative solutions to this important problem? If not, this can mean not only a decline in the viability and the respectability of public administration and MA, but it could also mean the decline of our civilization.

NOTES

1. Vincent Ostrom, *The Intellectual Crisis in American Public Administration* (University, AL: The University of Alabama Press, 1974), p. 10.

2. H. George Frederickson, *New Public Administration* (University, AL: The University of Alabama Press, 1980), pp. x–xii.

3. Ibid., p. 122.

4. Ibid.

5. Ibid., p. xi.

6. Ibid., p. xii.

7. Herbert Kaufman, "Administrative Decentralization and Political Power," *Public Administration Review* (Washington, D.C.: ASPA, Jan./Feb. 1969): 3–15.

8. H. George Frederickson, *New Public Administration* (University, AL: The University of Alabama Press, 1980), p. 5.

9. Ibid., p. 6.

10. Ibid., p. 8.

11. Herbert Kaufman, "Administrative Decentralization and Political Power," *Public Administration Review* (Washington, D.C.: ASPA, Jan./Feb. 1969): 14.

12. Dwight Waldo, "Some Thoughts on Alternatives, Dilemmas, and Paradoxes in a Time of Turbulence," *Public Administration in a Time of Turbulence* (New York, N.Y.: Chandler Publishing, 1971), p. 264.

13. Ibid., p. 267.

14. Ibid., p. 261.

15. Ibid., p. 270.

16. H. George Frederickson, *New Public Administration* (University, AL: The University of Alabama Press, 1980), p. 9.

17. Dwight Waldo, "Some Thoughts on Alternatives, Dilemmas, and Paradoxes in a Time of Turbulence," *Public Administration in a Time of Turbulence* (New York, N.Y.: Chandler Publishing, 1971), p. 274.

18. Leonard Greenhalgh and Robert McKersie, "Cost-Effectiveness of Alternative Strategies for Cut-back Management," *Public Administration Review* (Washington, D.C.: ASPA, Nov./Dec. 1980): 9.

19. Dwight Waldo, *The Enterprise of Public Administration* (Novato, CA: Chandler and Sharp Publishers, 1980), pp. 158–161.

20. Richard Schott, "Public Administration as a Profession: Problems and Prospects," *Public Administration Review* (Washington, D.C.: ASPA, May/June 1976): 254.

21. H. George Frederickson, *New Public Administration* (University, AL: The University of Alabama Press, 1980), p. 18.

22. Vincent Ostrom and Elinor Ostrom, "Public Choice: A Different Approach to the Study of Public Administration," *Public Administration Review* (Washington, D.C.: ASPA, March/April 1971), p. 205.

23. H. George Frederickson, *New Public Administration* (University, AL: The University of Alabama Press, 1980), p. 106.

24. Richard Pascale and Anthony Athens, *The Art of Japanese Management* (New York, N.Y.: Simon and Schuster, 1981), p. 204.

APPENDIX A

Research Process

The steps in research process were as follows:

1. The head of the randomly selected MA unit was contacted over the phone, the research project was described briefly, and an appointment was scheduled.

2. During the meeting with the unit head the research project was described in more detail and the official's go-ahead to conduct the research was established. General information was collected about the MA unit, such as its philosophy, organization, and functions, and any current hot topics. Many of the MA officers were willing to spend considerable time discussing their unit, the larger agency, and their philosophy of management and management analysis.

In the second phase of the meeting, studies conducted by the MA units were discussed and those meeting the research criteria were selected. The largest MA study meeting the criteria was chosen for further examination. The researcher then obtained the name of the analyst who conducted the study, the name of the decision maker who received it, and a copy of the written study report.

3. An appointment was arranged with the analyst who conducted the study for detailed interview (see Appendix B) for the structured interview guide. In most cases two interviews were conducted with each analyst because of the amount of information collected. Interviews were also conducted with decision makers for most of the studies.

4. The written study report was reviewed using the document review guide (see Appendix C).

APPENDIX B

Interview Guide

I. Problem Definition:
   A. Content
      1. What was the problem? Answers to this question are expected to be unique and may not be classified or grouped in any fashion.
      2. What was the purpose of the study? To assist in making a specific decision; to define the problem; to determine the severity of the problem; to structure the problem; to gain acceptance in one part of the organization for a decision made in another part.
      3. Was the problem structured? Not structured, structured by describing relationships in narrative; descriptive model; quantitative relationships among variables; predictive model.
   B. Process
      1. Who asked for the study? Bureau director; associate director for administration; division chief of unit being studied; management analysis division chief; the executive board; the administrative officers; unclear.
      2. Who defined the problem? The person requesting the study; the management analyst; team of analysts; interunit study team; both the analyst and the person requesting the study; the management analyst and personnel in the unit being studied.
      3. By what process was the problem defined? By the decision maker alone; by the analyst individually; by an interunit

study team; by meetings between the analyst and the decision maker; by meeting between the analyst and personnel in the unit studied; by a written memo from the director.

II. Information (Data) Collection:
  A. Content
    1. What methods were used in information collection? Manuals and written documentation; literature review; unstructured interviews; structured interviews; unstructured questionnaire; structured questionnaire; statistical sampling; participant observation; examination of existing office records; narrative, statistical; examination of accounting records; statistical sampling, gathering of empirical statistical data, experimental.
    2. What kind of information was collected? Oral comments in interviews; narrative comments on questionnaires; qualitative data from secondary sources; quantitative data from secondary sources; numbers—statistics; dollar costs—dollar benefits; experimental.
  B. Process
    1. Who collected the information (data)? The analyst; team of analysts; members of interunit study team; the chief in the unit being studied; the analyst and the head of the unit being studied; a joint effort between the analyst and the personnel in the unit being studied; personnel in the unit studied.
    2. How was it decided what information would be collected? By the analyst alone; by a team of analysts; by an interunit study team; by the analyst in consultation with the chief of the unit being studied; by the analyst in consultation with personnel in the unit being studied.

III. Information (Data) Analysis and Interpretation
  A. Content
    1. How was the information organized, analyzed and interpreted? The information was not summarized, raw data were used; information was summarized in narrative; the costs and benefits were described in narrative fashion; a count was made of the pro and con comments; the costs were quantified in dollars; costs and benefits were quantified in dollars.
    2. What methods were used to organize, analyze, and interpret the data? None, only raw data were used; the intuition and judgment of the analyst; the arithmetic mean was computed; descriptive statistics; cost analysis; inferential statistics; a

benefit/cost model; present-value analysis; correlation; regression.

B. Process
1. Who organized, analyzed, and interpreted the data? The analysts; a team of analysts; the interunit study team; the unit chief who requested the study; the analyst and the chief of the unit studied; the analyst and personnel in the unit studied.
2. How was it decided how the data would be ordered, analyzed, and interpreted? By the analyst alone; by a team of analysts in meetings; by an interunit study team; by a statistics consultant; by the analyst in consultation with the chief of the unit studied; by the analyst in consultation with personnel in the unit studied.

IV. Development of Conclusions and Recommendations
A. Content
1. What conclusions and recommendations were developed? This answer will be specific to each study and answers may not be able to be classified.
2. What was the basis for the conclusions and recommendations? Recommendations were based on a statistical analysis of the data; recommendations were obvious from narrative information; were obvious from numerical data; consultation with decision makers; consultation between the analyst and unit chief; the division chief and analyst jointly worked out the recommendations using their own judgment; consultation between the analyst and personnel in the unit studied.

B. Process
1. Who developed the conclusions and recommendations? The analyst; a team of analysts; the analyst in consultation with the chief of the unit studied; interunit study team; the management analyst and personnel in the unit studied.
2. By what process were the conclusions and recommendations developed? The analyst working alone; a team of analysts together; the analyst in consultation with the chief of the unit studied; an interunit study team; the analyst and personnel in the unit studied.

Answers to these questions will be provided by interviews, information in the written study report, and backup materials developed in the study. A list of suggested documents to examine includes background material initiating the study, the study plan, work sheets or backup material not included in the study report, the study report, itself, and any follow-up materials developed after the study report was completed.

APPENDIX C _____

Document Review Guide

The purpose of the document review guide is to focus the researcher's examination of MA study reports on the research questions. The kind of information gathered in the document review is very similar to that called for in interviews with the analysts who conducted the study. Each study report will be reviewed prior to the interview with the analyst. The review of the report will familiarize the researcher with the study and, also, provide a check for information collected in the interview.

Study reports will contain information relevant to two of the three major areas to be examined: the kind of study and the methods used in conducting the study. Information about the acceptance and implementation of recommendations is typically not included in reports. Study recommendations, of course, are included in reports.

The procedure for examining the study reports will be as follows:

1. The researcher will classify the study as to kind using the typology that has been developed.

2. The researcher will describe the methods used in the conduct of the study using the typology for study methods. It is expected that most study reports will provide only partial information about methodology. Most of the information about study methods will come from interviews.

3. The recommendations contained in the report will be classified using the typology of recommendations.

APPENDIX D

A Taxonomy for Policy Analysis

The table following this narrative presents a complete taxonomy of the field of policy analysis, a field in which management analysts are frequent practitioners. This is the first attempt known to us that such a classification scheme, including appropriate reference material, has been developed for this field.

This taxonomy has several possible uses: as a guide to define the field of policy analysis; as a guide to study for comprehensive exams; as a tool to determine possible areas for research; and as a tool to apply theoretical concepts into practical applications.

It is important to stress that this taxonomy covers both the theoretical scope of policy analysis as well as the practical scope. The theoretical scope includes such issues as the possible approaches to policy analysis, analytical techniques, and boundaries. The practical scope includes the use of policy analysis in government, how it is produced and used, and the institutionalization of policy analysis.

Two points need to be made about the reference documents. First, this reference material is not intended to cover everything written about the subject, but to provide readers with a cogent introduction to the subject with a moderate amount of depth. Second, it is necessary to explain how to interpret the numbers listed under references. The first number (between semicolons) represents the title of the book or article, which can be found in the back of the taxonomy. Other numbers after the dash represent page numbers in the book or article. For example, (6–17; 5–172–178; 10–11, 12, 13) should be interpreted to read page 17 of the 6th book, pages 172–178 of the fifth book, and pages 11, 12, and 13 of the 10th book.

Subject

References

I. Theoretical Scope of Policy Analysis (PA)

A. Definition of PA (What is PA?) — 4-222, 223; 10-ix, 7, 35; 17-4, 21; 18-1, 3; 20-5; 22-2.

  1. Boundaries of PA — 2-383; 4-260, 261; 12-200.

  2. Disciplines contributing to PA — 10-36; 12-197; 20-175; 4-223.

B. General Model of PA (How to Accomplish) — 10-363; 15-5, 6; 16-56; 17-20, 50.

C. Approaches to PA — 6-1; 7-83.

  1. Fundamental Approaches

    a. Rational — 10-226, 230; 4-226; 6-117-125, 211-227; 13-14, 15; 19-9.

    b. Incremental — 6-125-129, 189-211; 7-75; 79; 10-226; 11-86, 94; 16-271, 272; 17-28, 30; 19-11.

    c. Mixed Scanning — 6-129-134, 227-230; 10-231; 19-12.

    d. General Systems — 6-134-140, 230-252.

    e. Learning-Adaptive (Clinical) — 6-140-146, 252-285.

  2. Time Dimension — 10-51.

    a. Prospective

    b. Retrospective

    c. Integrated

  3. Basic Orientation

    a. Empirical — 10-36-38.

181

REFERENCE INDEX

1. "Policy Analysis in the Bureaucracy," Vitecitti, J. P., *Public Administration Review* 42 (Sept./Oct. 1982): 466–474.

2. "Paradigms of Public Administration," Nicholas Henry, *Public Administration Review* 35 (July/August 1975): 378–386.

3. "On the Organization of Inquiry: A Comparison of Some Radically Different Approaches to Public Administration," Ian I. Mitroff and Louis R. Pondy, *Public Administration Review* 34 (Sept./Oct. 1974): 471–479.

4. "Symposium on Policy Analysis in Government," *Public Administration Review* 37 (May/June 1977) Norman Beckman (Ed.): 221–310.

6. *The National Planning Idea in U.S. Public Policy,* David E. Wilson (Boulder, Colo.: Westview Press, 1980).

10. *Public Policy Analysis,* William Dunn (Englewood Cliffs, N.J.: Prentice-Hall, 1981).

11. *A Strategy of Decision,* David Braybrooke and Charles Lindblom (New York: New York Free Press, 1970).

12. "Policy Analysts: A New Professional Role in Government Service," Yehezkel Dror, *Public Administration Review* 27 (Sept. 1967): 197–203.

14. "Problems and Prospects for Policy Evaluation," Frank Scioli, Jr., *Public Administration Review* 39 (Jan./Feb., 1979): 41–45.

15. *A Primer for Policy Analysis,* Edith Skokey and Richard Zeckhauser (New York: W. W. Norton, 1978).

16. *The Art of Public Policy Analysis,* Peter House (Beverly Hills: Sage Publications, 1981).

17. *Analysis for Public Decisions,* E. S. Quade (New York: North Holland Press, 1982).

18. *Policy Analysis,* Thomas Dye (Tuscaloosa, Alabama: University of Alabama Press, 1976).

19. *Public Policy-Making,* James Anderson (New York: Rinehart and Winston, 1984).

20. *The Policy-Studies Handbook,* Stuart Nagel (Lexington, Mass.: Lexington Books, 1980).

21. *Policy Analysts in the Bureaucracy,* Arnold Meltsner (Berkeley: University of California Press, 1976).

Annotated Bibliography

Afzal, Mohammad. "Management Analysis; An Emerging Staff Function." Unpublished doctoral dissertation, Cornell University, Ithaca, N.Y., June 1962.

In October 1960, the Office of the Chief of Engineers directed certain employees to undertake the following tasks during the forthcoming fiscal year of 1961:

1. Devise ways and means to get more effective contractor participation in accident prevention on construction contracts. Prepare detailed outline of procedures to be followed.

2. Make sampling evaluation of supervisors and employees to determine awareness of and effectiveness in carrying out personnel management responsibilities.

3. Develop check lists for budgeting data preparation and review.

4. Prepare a comprehensive report of the problem of assignment of supply contracts, and recommend possible improvements.

5. Study feasibility and practicability of applying work simplification to clerical employees.

6. Study practicability and economic justification of microfilming field note books for record purposes.

It is significant that the employees concerned were not part of the line organization of the Corps of Engineers, but were members of a distinct staff group specializing in studying, analyzing, and suggesting ways and means to improve management in their corps. Nor were the above problems all; they constituted only some six out of 99 similar tasks assigned to the same staff personnel.

The work of such personnel, whose role and functions have been developing over the last several decades and gaining stature with the growth of complex modern organization and technology, is the subject of this study. These employees and their functions have been described by various terms at different times and in different organizations and countries. This study, however, uses the nomenclature current in the U.S. federal government, which is "management analysis."

This dissertation provides a comprehensive review of the evolution and emergence of management analysis as a staff function in the federal government. The beginnings of management analysis from 1880 to 1920 are discussed, and its evolution from 1920 to 1960 is described. Topics covered in this review and analysis of management analysis include its development and scope in federal agencies, analytical tools, organization and methods (O&M) in Canada and Great Britain, and major concerns and issues in the professional field.

Brown, David S. "The Management Analyst: Who is He and What Does He Do?" Mimeograph, Department of Public Administration, George Washington University, Washington, D.C.
This interesting paper describes who the analyst is, his place in the organization, and his academic background and personal characteristics. Over twenty activities that management analysts perform are discussed.

Buetow, C. Peter. "Management Analysis and Decisionmaking." *CA Magazine* (Canada) 111, no. 8 (August 1978): 90, 92.
A distinction can and should be made between analysis and decision making. Analysis defines the problem and determines what solutions are available, along with the attributes of each. Decision making concerns comparing the alternatives and giving each a weight based on corporate strategy and philosophy, as well as determining the risk factors involved. The decision maker must try to determine if all the alternatives have been considered by the analyst. Exclusion of some alternatives could lead to selection of a predetermined solution. The true decision-making process is selection from alternatives, and it is a managerial process. The process starts with a definition of objectives that will not result in a justification procedure for any activity. Possible bias on the part of the analyst should not be overlooked.

Kfir, Aharon. "Government Reorganization: An Analysis of Selected Organization Studies Carried Out by Organization and Methods Units in Israel." Unpublished doctoral dissertation, Syracuse University, 1969.
Two considerations of major interest to researchers and writers on government reorganization are understanding the actual mechanism of reorganization and advocating effective methods for reorganization. As a result of this probing, several approaches to organization study—the main stage in the organization process—have been developed and utilized in many countries.
Reorganizations have been carried out in the Israeli government ever since the establishment of the state in 1948. Recently, organization and methods (O&M) units have become established as an accepted way of carrying out organization studies.
The purpose of the dissertation is to describe and examine the main aspects

of organization studies performed by O&M units in Israel, with two objectives in mind. First, in a narrow sense, analysis of the main aspects of government organization studies in Israel is used to construct a descriptive model that will facilitate understanding of the process and some of the dimensions involved. Second, in a wider sense, the purpose of the dissertation is to point out the shortcomings of existing approaches to government reorganization utilized by the O&M units in Israel. Achievement of these objectives will serve as a basis to argue the need for improvements in both the general theoretical basis of government reorganization and in the capability of O&M units to carry out more-effective organization studies.

The analysis is based upon data collected in eighteen units within the Israeli government where organization studies have been carried out by O&M officers. The investigation relies mainly on field interviews with people involved and on examination of records. These have been supported by the author's personal observations and participation in some of the studies. The field research was carried out within a conceptual framework based on relevant literature on government reorganization.

The study emphasizes the role of implicit goals in initiating, supporting, and implementing organization studies. It also shows the limitations of the structural approach to reorganization, the scope of the mission stated, the activities performed, the recommendations made and implemented, and the impact on the effectiveness of the organizations in the organization studies carried out by O&M units in Israel. Based on these findings, the study argues that the existing approaches to government reorganization in Israel do not provide a good model for the study of organization and that O&M units in Israel in their present state do not have the capability to perform effective organization studies.

Future research is proposed on two subjects. First, utilization of available knowledge drawn from modern organization and general systems theory, in order to develop an integrated and more comprehensive approach to government reorganization; and second, enhancement of the capability of O&M units to carry out more-effective organization studies. Some guidelines to these two proposed subjects for future research are given in the two approaches.

Laframboise, H. L. "Administration Inspections and Methods Analysis in the Department of Veterans Affairs." *Canadian Public Administration* 2 (December 1959): 195–201.

This article assesses the differences and similarities between inspection and organization and methods (O&M) work and presents an approach for how they can be successfully combined. The primary concern of an inspector is to determine if the operations under examination conform to preestablished standards, while the main focus of the O&M officer is an examination of the rules themselves. The author concludes that the combination of field inspection and methods analysis can be successfully established in any organization with extensive field operations provided that certain limited conditions are met.

Lloyd, Iris M. "Don't Define the Problem." *Public Administration Review* (May/June 1978): 283–286.

The thesis of this paper is that management analysis of very complex problems may be facilitated if the effort to formulate a thoroughgoing definition of the problem is delayed or even omitted from the analysis. Attempts to define a very complex and dynamic problem may result in an oversimplified or erroneous definition which, in turn, leads to an irrelevant solution. The approach this paper proposes is to experiment with tentative solutions and, by observing the results, arrive at an understanding of the problem.

Lyngseth, D. M. "The Use of Organization and Methods in Canadian Government." *Canadian Public Administration* 4, no. 4 (December 1962): 428–492.

This excellent article is based on master's thesis research conducted at Carleton University. Information on the O&M function (called *management analysis* in the United States) in Canadian federal and provincial governments and crown corporations was collected by questionnaires and interviews. The article explores a wide range of questions that can be asked of O&M including the need for O&M, what it is, what services are provided, and what methods and techniques are used.

A brief history of the O&M function in Britain since it was begun in 1914 and in the United States is presented. The initiation and development of O&M in Canada is described in considerable detail, including each federal department and crown corporation. O&M in provincial and municipal governments is also discussed. Other interesting topics treated include government O&M units vs. private consultants, compulsory vs. adversary O&M, and the organizational location of O&M units. A tabulation of the number of O&M units providing twelve major O&M services is presented. The article concludes with a discussion of the characteristics of O&M personnel, O&M as seen through the eyes of a prospective employee, and training practices.

Melrose, E. D. "Organization and Methods." *Public Administration* 38 (Summer 1960): 119–30.

This excellent article describes the evolution of growth of the organization and methods (O&M) function in England. Some of the main ideas discussed include the recognition of a need for O&M and its beginning, where O&M fits into an organization, the personal traits required for O&M work, where the new "O&M unit should first cut its teeth," and approaches to carrying out assignments successfully.

Nadel, M. V., and C. M. Kerwin. "Management and Organizational Assessments: A Review of Selected Organizations." Battelle Human Affairs Research Centers, Washington, D.C., February 1984.

The report reviews the processes and criteria used by organizations other than the Nuclear Regulatory Commission (NRC) in conducting management and organization audits and evaluations. As part of a larger project assisting the NRC in establishing improved procedures and guidelines for assessing the management and organization of applicants for nuclear power plant operating licenses, this report provides a comparative perspective on organizational assessment. The organizations whose management audits are reviewed are state public utility commissions, the Comptroller of the Currency, the Department of Health and Human Services' Office of Health Maintenance Organizations, the Food and Drug Administration, the General Accounting Office, and a large commercial insurance company. This report examines the purposes, areas of emphasis, and processes used in these reviews.

Oman, Ray C. "The Nature, Conduct and Acceptance of Management Analysis Studies in Civilian Federal Agencies." Unpublished doctoral dissertation, The George Washington University, Washington, D.C., 1983.

Thousands of specialists conduct studies to provide information and analysis for management decisions in the federal government. These include 40,000 economists, industrial engineers, management analysts, operations research analysts, and program analysts. Management analysts compose the largest analytical job series, numbering about a third of the total. They are charged with improving organization efficiency and effectiveness, and their studies are the focus of this research.

While management analysts conduct a large number of studies to assist in decision making each year, little information exists about the nature or effectiveness of these efforts. This research documents the nature of the studies conducted. It also explores the relationships between kinds of studies and methods and processes used and the acceptance of recommendations. Two-hour interviews were conducted with fifty analysts and decision makers in fifteen selected agencies throughout the government. Detailed typologies were developed to describe studies and to provide a basis for testing concepts about acceptance.

One major finding was that the most common type of study was of work methods and procedures (one-third of the cases) and was conducted by descriptive methods. Another major finding was that selected characteristics of the nature, methodology, and process of studies, as well as larger organization factors, were related to acceptance. A tabular analysis of study characteristics, facts about each study gathered in interviews, and opinions of analysts and decision makers each suggested somewhat different factors influencing acceptance. For example, the tabular analysis suggested that the kind of study and recommendations were important factors affecting acceptance, while study methods and processes also had some effect. Factual data collected in interviews pointed to larger organization happenings, such as the change of political administrations, as important factors influencing acceptance. Analysts and decision makers believed the content of recommendations as well as events in the organization environment were key factors affecting acceptance.

Some particular findings are that the duration of the study, the organization location, and the number of organization units covered by the recommendations influence acceptance. In addition, acceptance is influenced by quantitative versus qualitative approaches, solitary versus participative study processes, and whether individual analysts, teams of analysts, or interunit teams conducted the study. The research suggests that many aspects of studies are within the control of the analyst and may be used to increase acceptance.

Oman, Ray C., and LTC Sam L. Lyles. "Management Analysis in the Federal Government." *Armed Forces Comptroller* 28, no. 4 (Fall 1983): 12–17.

The functions, activities, and roles of management analysts in the federal government are discussed. The development and evolution of management analysis over the past thirty years is described along with information on the numbers and organizational distribution of analysts. Conclusions about the field of management analysis are drawn based on interviews with management analysis officers.

Oman Ray C., and Stephen R. Chitwood. "Management Evaluation Studies: Factors Affecting Acceptance of Recommendations." *Evaluation Review* 8, no. 3 (June 1984): 283–305.

This article summarizes the results of in-depth research conducted about the many management evaluations performed in the federal government each year. Little information exists about the nature or effectiveness of these evaluations even though they cost more than $200 million annually. The article explores the relationships between kinds of evaluations, analytic methods, and interpersonal processes and the acceptance of recommendations by decision makers. Detailed typologies based on a review of the literature provide the basis for quantitatively testing concepts about the utilization of evaluation against empirical data. Two-hour interviews were conducted with fifty evaluators and decision makers about randomly selected management evaluations. Selected characteristics of the nature, methodology, and process of evaluations were found to be related to acceptance. Some factors are structural and beyond the control of the evaluator, while others are behavioral and within the power of the evaluator to influence.

Padilla, Perfecto L. "Organization and Methods Practices in the Governments of Canada and the Philippines: A Comparative Study." Unpublished masters thesis, Carleton University, Canada, 1965.

This thesis presents a comparative description and analysis of organization and methods (O&M) practices in the governments of Canada and the Philippines.

Canadian and Philippine experiences in organization and management improvement are compared on the basis of controversial issues and significant problems pertaining to the theory and practice of government O&M. Among the more important issues examined is the organization and management of O&M in which the two governments have striking similarities and differences. One chapter attempts a fairly extensive analytical treatment of the organizational location and internal operations of the central O&M staff in each government, the establishment of departmental O&M units, and their relationships with the central body.

In a discussion of how the O&M staff in each government carries out their work, certain issues are brought up such as initiation of a management study, importance of defining terms of reference, conflict between management principles and practical approach to problem situations, and responsibility for implementation of recommendations.

The activities and accomplishments of each government in the O&M field are described, and an evaluation of these accomplishments is attempted. The author also examines the problems affecting the practice of O&M in the two governments under review. And in the concluding chapter, O&M trends and its future in Canadian and Philippine public administration are examined.

Pitman, I. J. "Organization and Methods." *Public Administration* 26 (1948): 1–9.

This article documents the beginning and evolution of the O&M function in the British government. The MacDonald Report in 1914 gave the first official recognition to the organization and methods function, but it was with Sir Horace Wilson and Mr. Reid-Young in 1941 that emphasis on all the appropriate aspects of O&M were pulled together. "The Office Machines Section of the Treasury, founded in 1919, historically was the beginning of O&M." A significant milestone occurred in 1941 when the Reid-Young memorandum stated "a clear recognition of the need to shed the function of negative control and to develop a new function of positive initiation." The article discusses the growth and spread of the O&M function through the ministries of the British government between 1942 and 1947.

Price, David Sutherland. "In Quest of Administrative Improvement: Organization and Methods in Egypt, 1955–59." Unpublished doctoral dissertation, State University of New York at Albany, 1963.
Developing lands, eager for swift attainment of goals, seek outside assistance. Organization and methods, through rational attention to government structure and procedure, offers one approach toward administrative improvement. Technical assistance in public administration encourages the development of national solutions on the premise that western techniques cannot be transplanted into transitional cultures without adaptation. Visiting experts and programs, proclaiming the truth of the premise, depart from it in practice. All too often, O&M aims homeland instruction at foreign problems, and needs are not served effectively. Egyptian administration, personalized and centralized, faces population pressure, poverty, citizen nonparticipation, and emergent nationalism rising from a foreign-dominated past.

An Institute of Public Administration was established in 1954, with United Nations participation. O&M programs from 1955 to 1959 train many men, see the beginnings of central and ministry O&M offices, and lead to some modest project successes. Western instruction and techniques are misunderstood and inappropriate in many instances. The doctrine of public administration counterparts is impracticable for Egypt, and many nationals are used in assistantship roles.

The concluding chapter presents recommendations to increase the effectiveness of O&M toward administrative improvement. Of general applicability to developing lands are suggestions that the adaptation of the expert to the overseas culture and administrative system is of paramount importance and that this can be advanced through selection emphasizing versatility and adaptability. Suggestions of specific applicability to Egypt in 1960 include continuation of O&M training on a broad base but careful limitation of selection of men for O&M offices, some modifications in O&M training content and method, and manifestation of increased management support in establishing programs, appointing personnel and chiefs free from concurrent assignments, ensuring timely consideration of recommendations, and encouraging modest rather than omnibus projects. Continuing United Nations provision of an expert in O&M is not recommended.

Public Administration. "O&M—How It All Began." 27 (Spring 1949): 45–46.
This article reviews the Pitman article that appeared in the previous (26

[Spring 1948]) issue of *Public Administration,* clarifies and refines facts, and presents an alternative interpretation of the beginnings of O&M.

Sherman, Harvey. "Realistic Objectives for Internal Consulting." Paper presented at the 9th Annual Conference of the Association of Internal Management Consultants, Sea Island, Georgia, June 2, 1980.
This readable and interesting paper discusses the limitations of organizations, consultants, and concepts of consulting, and by the process of declaration provides valuable advice to the internal consultant.

Somowijoto, Sunarno. "The Role and The Function of an Organization and Methods Unit in a Government Department: A Case Study in the Department of Agriculture of the Republic of Indonesia." Unpublished masters thesis, American University, Washington, D.C., 1982.
Organization and Methods units, management tools to increase administrative efficiency, were introduced in 1974 in all government departments in Indonesia. In addition, 724 personnel have been trained in O&M techniques, yet O&M units are less effective, generally speaking, than they should be in aiding the departments to fulfill their constituent tasks.

This thesis is intended to develop a model of an O&M unit and find the potential for implementing this model in the Indonesian government department. Of the various available models, the model proposed by Harris is the most applicable and adaptable.

However, due to the rigidity of the current administrative system this model still cannot be implemented. Lembaga Administrasi Negara (LAN) as the functional agency in improving government administration should review the current system and evaluate the model's potential in that context.

U.S. Agency Management Analysis Officers Group. "The General Management Analyst: A Concept of the Character of the Occupation." March 1960.
This paper provides a conceptual framework for the management analyst occupation in the federal government. The character of the management analysis staff function is described. The knowledge, skills, abilities, and personal characteristics required of management analysis are discussed.

U.S. Department of Army, Army Regulation 5–3. *Comptroller—Deputy Chief of Staff for Resource Management Functional Responsibilities,* November 1986.
This publication prescribes the army's standard installation organization and describes installation management principles and responsibilities. It also provides guidelines for organizing activities at the installation level.

U.S. Department of the Army, Office of the Chief of Engineers, ER 5–1–7. *Efficiency Reviews Program,* September 1986.
This regulation establishes policies, procedures, and responsibilities for implementing the Corps of Engineer Efficiency Reviews Program.

U.S. Department of the Army, Office of the Chief of Engineers, ER 1–1–90. *Management Analysis Activities of Management Analysis Branches,* January 1964.
This regulation establishes policy and guidance for the management branches of all field agencies of the Corps of Engineers in performing their

management analysis, management assistance, and management engineering responsibilities.

U.S. Bureau of the Budget. "Management Analysis at the Headquarters of Federal Agencies: An Inventory of Agency Practices Concerning the Staff Function of Management Analysis." October 1959.

This in-depth and informative report is the product of a Bureau of Budget study of management analysis staff function in headquarters of federal agencies. Some of the topics addressed include "the problem of defining management analysis," agency concepts on the roles of management analysis, "the general management analysis unit," and the education and experience of professional analysts. The various work activities of management analysts are described, and the distribution of time spent on their activities is presented. Management studies emerged as the most important and time-taking activity.

Watts, Theodora Kinderman. "Management and Organization in Federal Agencies and Analysis of the Characteristics and Functionings of Boundary Spanning Personnel." Unpublished doctoral dissertation, American University, Washington, D.C., 1982.

The need for effective boundary agents in organizations increases as environmental turbulence increases. Traditionally, management and organization (M&O) units have served as boundary agents and efficiency experts in federal organizations. Today the M&O role requires a high level of boundary-spanning activity (BSA), which has not been formally acknowledged or rewarded.

A multilevel data gathering was used to ascertain the current status of M&O units, including both archival information and a mailed-out questionnaire to heads of M&O units throughout the government. The findings indicate that the work programs of M&O units have shifted toward increasing their administrative management activities—an increase of 225 percent over the 1959 figure. In addition, very little time is being committed to conducting long-term studies to improve operations; most studies are short-turnaround, problem-solving exercises.

A major problem for management analysts is the continuing conflict and ambiguity they experience as a consequence of their staff positions among line managers who are less than totally supportive. Evidence of chronic organizational stress was expected, but little was found, as both high levels of job satisfaction and low tension levels were reported. Four causal models based on previous research linking the study variables were evaluated, resulting in discarding two of the four models. The model containing a direct link between BSA and job satisfaction in addition to a link with tension explained the observed data better than the other models. This implies that increasing boundary-spanning activity not only increases satisfaction by reducing tension, but also directly increases job satisfaction.

At the organizational level the findings indicate that the M&O function is not being used as it was intended. Analytical work has been displaced by increased administrative management responsibilities, and staffing levels within the units are dropping, compounding the erosion of the resources available for analytical work. Because reducing the analytical capabilities of an organization impairs its ability to adapt to environmental changes, we can expect the changes within M&O units to affect negatively our federal agencies' long-term health and viability.

White, M. J. "Top Management and Management Science: An Exploratory Study in 15 Federal Civilian Agencies." Paper presented at the National Conference of the American Society for Public Administration, Denver, April 18–21, 1971.

This is a study of the relation between top managers in federal agencies and the operations research and management science (OR/MS) group. Sixteen managers were questioned about the following characteristics: closeness of top managers to OR/MS groups, top managers' attitudes toward the OR/MS activities, relation between closeness and these attitudes, and top managers' use of OR/MS groups. It is concluded that OR/MS is relevant to many top managers and that OR/MS has begun to play a role in decisions. Top management attitudes and actions are not related in obvious ways. The consequences to top management's use of and closeness to an OR/MS group need not be the success of the group as a professional, innovative, research-oriented unit.

Selected Bibliography

Archibald, K. A. "Three Views of the Expert's Role in Policymaking: Systems Analysis, Incrementalism, and the Clinical Approach." *Policy Sciences* 1 (1970): 73–86.

Argyris, Chris, and Donald Schon. *Theory in Practice: Increasing Professional Effectiveness*. Washington, D.C.: Jossey-Bass, 1977.

Bahnert, Lea Mallison. "Federal Administrative Analysis Offices." Unpublished doctoral dissertation, University of Chicago, August 1947.

Baker, John K. "Making Staff Consulting More Effective." *Harvard Business Review* (Jan.-Feb., 1969) 62–71.

Bean, Alden Suydam. "Management Science—Client Relationships: Studies of Linking Mechanisms." Unpublished dissertation, Northwestern University, Evanston, Illinois, August 1972.

Cox, Gary B. "Managerial Style: Implications for the Utilization of Program Evaluation Information." *Evaluation Quarterly* 1, no. 3 (August 1977): 444–509.

Crozier, Michael. *The Bureaucratic Phenomenon*. Chicago: University of Chicago Press, 1964.

Davis, Howard R., and Susan E. Salasin. "The Utilization of Evaluation." In *Handbook of Evaluation Research,* Elmer L. Struening and Marcia Guttentag, eds., Beverly Hills: Sage Publications, vol. 1, 1975, pp. 621–666.

Dovey, H. O. *Handbook of Organization and Methods Techniques*. Brussels: International Institute of Administration Sciences, 1960.

Downs, Anthony. "Some Thoughts on Giving People Economic Advice." *American Behavioral Scientist* 9, no. 1 (September 1965): 30–32.

Dror, Yehezkel. "Applied Social Science and Systems Analysis." *Public Administration Review* (September 1967): 109–132.

Dyckman, Thomas. "Management Implementation of Scientific Research: An Attitudinal Study." *Management Science* 13 (1967): B612-B620.

Emmerich, H. "Administrative Systems and Methods." Institute of Public Administration, *Proceedings,* 1952.

Etzioni, Amitai. "Two Approaches to Organization Analysis." *Administrative Science Quarterly* 5, no. 2 (1960): 1–15.

Fisher, John E. "Do Federal Managers Manage?" *Public Administration Review* 22 (Spring 1962): 59–64.

Fite, H. H. "Evaluating the Work of Office Methods Staff." *Organization and Methods Bulletin* 12, no. 4 (August 1957).

Flanders, Loretta R. "Program Evaluation: Merging Practical and Methodological Consideration." *The Bureaucrat* 7, no. 3 (Fall 1978): 43–49.

Forester, John. "The Practice of Evaluation and Policy Analysis." Working Paper No. 257, Berkeley, Department of City and Regional Planning, University of California, July 1975.

Gardner, C. James. "Organization and Methods Development in the Government of Canada." *Public Administration* 36 (Spring 1977): 283–316.

Gibson, G. H. "What I Expect from O&M." *Public Administration* 36 (Summer 1958): 169–71.

Gladieux, Bernard L., "Administrative Planning in the Federal Government." In *Process of Organization and Management,* Catheryn Seckler-Hudson, ed. Washington, D.C.: The American University Press, 1957 (pp. 171–188).

Glaser, Edward M., and Thomas E. Baker. "A Clinical Approach to Program Evaluation." *Evaluation* (Fall 1972): pp. 54–59.

Great Britain. House of Commons, Select Committee on Estimates: *Organization and Methods and Its Effect on the Staffing of Government Departments,* Fifth Report. Session 1946–47. London, 1947.

Gulick, Luther, and Lyndall Urwick, eds. *Papers on the Science of Administration.* New York: Institute of Public Administration, 1937.

Hammond, John S. "The Roles of the Manager and Management Scientist in Successful Implementation." *Sloan Management Review* 15, no. 2 (Winter 1974): 1–24.

Harris, Naville. "Research in Education: The Management Service Education." *Management Service* (July 1977): 1–13.

H. M. Treasury. Organization and Methods Division. *The Practice of O&M.* London, 1954.

Hooley, Megan. "O&M: Advisory of Executive?" *O&M Bulletin* 6 (October 1951).

Institute of Public Service and Foreign Administrators Training Program, The University of Connecticut (Storrs), "Papers from the First Annual Conference on The Role of Management Analysis in Government," May 27, 1964.

Jackson, G. T. "Management Improvement in the Canadian Civil Service." *Public Personnel Review* 12, no. 3 (July 1951).

Jebens, Arthur B., "Management Analysis, Its Past, Present, and Future." In Proceedings of the U.S. Bureau of the Budget Management Officers and Conference on Manpower Utilization and Management Improvement, Harpers Ferry, West Virginia, June 8–12, 1964 (8–14).

Johnston, William P., Jr., and Ray C. Oman. "Overcoming Resistance to

Change: Theory and Practice Provide Some Insights," *Knowledge Creation, Diffusion, Utilization* 11, no. 3 (March 1990): 268–279.

Kingdom, Thomas Doyle. *Improvement of Organization and Management in Public Administration*. Brussels: International Institute of Administrative Sciences, 1960.

Leonard, Herbert E., "A Study of the Scope and Organization of Management Analysis Programs in Federal Agencies." Unpublished masters thesis, The American University, Washington, D.C., February 1965.

Levitan, Laura C., and Edward F. X. Hughes. "Utilization of Evaluation: A Review and Synthesis." Working Paper No. 35, Department of Psychology, Evaluation and Methodology Center for Health Services and Policy Research, Northwestern University, Evanston, Illinois, January 1980.

Margulies, Newton. "Action Research and the Consultive Process." *Business Perspectives* (Fall 1968): 26–30.

Milward, George E. *Organization and Methods*. New York: St. Martin's Press, 1967.

Nottage, Raymond. "Organization and Methods in the Small Public Authority." *Public Administration* 32 (Summer 1954).

"O&M in the U.K. Central Government." *O&M Bulletin* 12, no. 4 (August 1957).

Oliver, Stanley. *O and M for the First-Line Managers*. London: Edward Arnold, 1975.

Patton, Michael Quinn. *Utilization Focused Evaluation*. Beverly Hills: Sage Publications, 1975.

Patton, Michael W., Patricia Smith Grimes, Kathryn M. Guthrie, Nancy J. Brennan, Barbara Dickey French, and Dale A. Blyth. "In Search of Impact: An Analysis of Utilization of Federal Health Evaluation Research." In *Using Social Research in Public Policy Making*, Carol H. Weiss, ed. Lexington, Mass.: Lexington Books, 1977.

Peter, Honora B. "Those Management Analysts." *The Washington Post*, August 4, 1981, A–14.

Quade, Edward S. *Analysis for Public Decisions*. New York: American Elsevier, 1975 (pp. 253–267).

Radnor, Michael, A. H. Rubenstein, and David Tansik. "Implementation of Operations Research in R&D in Government and Business Organizations." *Operations Research* 18 (Nov.-Dec. 1970): 967–991.

Rapp, William F. "Management Analysis at the Headquarters of Federal Agencies." *International Review of Administrative Sciences* 26, no. 3 (1960): 235–248.

Reisman, Arnold, and Cornelius A. de Kluyer. "Strategies for Implementing Systems Studies." In *Implementing Operations Research and Management Science*, Randall L. Schultz and Dennis P. Slevin, eds. New York: American Elsevier, 1975 (pp. 291–300).

Sauerborn, Willy. "Bonner Modell der Organisationsberatung-Methoden und Erfahrungen (The Bonn Model of Organization Advice-Methods and Experiences)." Verwaltungsfuehrung Organisation Personalwesen (Germany) 4 (July/August 1981): 209–212, 214–215.

Schultz, Randall L., and Dennis P. Slevin, eds. *Implementing Operations Research and Management Science.* New York: American Elsevier, 1975.

Schulberg, Herbert C., and Frank Baker. "Program Evaluations Models and the Implementation of Research Findings." *American Journal of Public Health* 58, no. 7 (July 1968): 1248–1255.

Seckler-Hudson, Catheryn. *Organization and Management: Theory and Practice.* Washington, D.C.: The American University Press, 1957.

Silverman, David. *The Theory of Organizations.* New York: Basic Books, 1971.

Tansik, David A. "Influence of Organization Goal Structures on the Selection and Implementation of Management Science Projects." In *Management and Policy Sciences in American Government,* Michael J. White et al. Lexington, Mass.: Lexington Books, 1965.

Thomas, Logan L. "Development of Organization and Methods in the United States." Unpublished doctoral dissertation, New York University, March 1950.

————, ed. *Processes of Organization and Management.* Washington, D.C.: Public Affairs Press, 1948.

Tullock, Gordon. *The Politics of Bureaucracy.* Washington, D.C.: Public Affairs Press, 1965.

U.S. Agency Management Analysis Officers Group. "The General Management Analyst: A Concept of the Character of the Occupation." March 1960.

U.S. Bureau of the Budget. "Directory of Projects: Management Research and Improvement." Compiled by Interagency Management Analysis Conference and Washington chapters of the Society for Advancement of Management and the American Society for Public Administration, November 1960.

————. "Organizational Placement and Nature of the Management Analysis Function." Report of a seminar task group, June 19–30, 1961.

————. "Management Analysis at the Headquarters of Federal Agencies: An Inventory of Agency Practices Concerning the Staff Function of Management Analysis." October 1959.

U.S. Department of Air Force, *"Wing/Base Level Management Analysis,"* Air Force Pamphlet No. 178–2, November, 1970.

U.S. Department of Air Force, Air Force Regulation 25–5, *Air Force Management Engineering Program of Management Advisory Services,* Vols. 1, 2, and 3, 1977.

U.S. Department of Commerce, Office of Organization and Management Systems. "Listing and Summary of Department of Commerce Management Reports, 1975–1977."

U.S. Office of Management and Budget. *Resources for Management Analysis.* Fiscal Year 1978.

————. *Resources for Program Evaluation.* Fiscal Year 1977.

U.S. Office of Personnel Management. *Federal Circular Workforce Statistics: Occupations of Federal White-Collar and Blue-Collar Workers.* October 31, 1985.

————. Position Classification Standards, TS 9, February, 1972.

————. Qualifications Standards, TS 141, February 1972.

Van de Vall, Mark D., and Cheryl Bolas. "The Utilization of Social Policy Research: An Empirical Analysis of Its Structure and Functions." 74th Annual Meeting of the American Sociology Association, Boston, August 27–31, 1979.

Van de Vall, Mark D., Cheryl Bolas, and Tai S. Kang. "Applied Social Research in Industrial Organizations: An Evaluation of Functions, Theory and Methods." *The Journal of Applied Behavioral Science* 12, no. 2 (April-May-June 1976): 159–177.

Vertlinsky, Ilan, Richard T. Barth, and Vance T. Mitchell. "A Study of ORMS Implementation—a Social Change Process." In *Implementing Operations Research and Management Science*, Randall L. Schultz and Dennis Slevin, eds. New York: American Elsevier, 1975 (pp. 253–270).

Wall, J. E. O. B. E. "The Plowden Report: IV. Management Service in Industry." *Public Administration* 41 (Spring 1963): 41–54.

Waller, John D. et al. *Developing Useful Evaluation Capability: Lessons from the Model Evaluation Program*. U.S. Department of Justice, Washington, D.C.: Government Printing Office, June, 1979.

Weber, Gustavus A. *Organized Efforts for the Improvement of Methods of Administration in the United States,* New York: D. Appleton, 1919.

Webster, W. A. R. *Handbook of O&M Analysis*. London: Business Book, 1973.

Weiss, Carol H. "Utilization of Evaluations—Toward Caomparative Study." In *Evaluation Action Programs*, Carol Weiss, ed. Boston: Allyn and Bacon, 1972.

————. "Between the Cup and the Lip," *Evaluation* Vol. 1, no. 2 (1973): 49–55.

White, Michael J., Michael Radnor, and David Tansik. *Management and Policy Science in American Government*. Lexington, Mass.: Lexington Books, 1975.

————. *Management Science in Federal Agencies,* Lexington, Mass.: D.C. Health, 1975.

————. "Analysis vs. Bargaining." Northwestern University, Evanston, Illinois, prepared for American Society for Public Administration Conference, Denver, April 18–21, 1971, for the panel addressing "Dilemmas of Policy Making in a Pluralistic Society."

————. "Operations Research, Organization Theory, and Public Policy Making." Cooperative International Program of Studies of Operations Research and the Management Sciences, Program Publication No. 8–71.

————. "The Impact of Management Science on Political Decision Making." Paper presented at the 66th Annual Meeting of the American Political Science Association, Los Angeles, Sept. 8–12, 1970.

Wholey, Joseph S. "What Can We Actually Get from Program Evaluation." *Policy Sciences* 3 (1972): 361–369.

Wildavsky, Aaron. "The Self-Evaluating Organization." *Public Administration Review* 32, no. 5 (September-October 1972): 509–520.

Windle, Charles, and Peter Bates. "Evaluating Program Evaluations." In *Eval-*

uations of Behavioral Programs in Community, Residential, and School Settings, by Park O. Davidson and Franklin W. Clark. Champaign, Ill.: Research Press, 1974.

Young, Carlotta, J. "Evaluation Research." Paper presented at the Evaluation Research Society Second Annual Meeting, Washington, D.C., November 2–4, 1978.

Index

Academic fields, relationships to management analysis, 11
"Ad hocracy," 38
Administration, 162
ADP (Automatic data processing). *See* Automation; Computers; Information resource management; Information systems
Advocacy, 164
Alternatives in policy analysis, 150
Analysis: examination of a sample of studies, 41–46; keys to successful studies, 91–107; the nature and acceptance of study recommendations, 109–131; an overview of studies, 15–21; studies, 2, 5–7; techniques of, 4. *See also* Benefit/cost analysis; Cost analysis; Economic analysis; Resource allocation
Analysis for decision making. *See* Decision making
Analysis for management, 2
Analytical staff jobs, 3
Analytical studies. *See* Management analysis studies; Studies
Applied behavioral science, 109–112
Art of Japanese Management, The, 168

Authority, 24, 25, 27, 28
Automation, 7, 63–77, 166; background of computers, 63; benefit/cost analysis, 69–73; costs, 69–73; decision-making criteria, 72–73; information resource management, 73–77; planning, 68–69; relationship to management analysis, 63–64; the role of management analysis in, 63–67; rules of thumb, 67; system life cycle, 67; training, 66; user needs, 67–68; user requirements, 67–68; value of information, 68. *See also* Computers; Information resource management; Information systems

Benefit/cost analysis (B/C), 3, 104–105, 148–149; of automation, 69–73; decision-making criteria, 81–82; marginal costs and benefits, 81–82; models of, 72–73; total factor productivity, 82. *See also* Cost analysis; Cost-effective (Cost-effectiveness); Decision making; Economic analysis
Benefits and costs. *See* Benefit/cost analysis; Cost analysis

About the Authors

RAY C. OMAN is a Senior Program Analyst with the Headquarters, U.S. Army Corps of Engineers, and has experience as an analyst and manager in both federal civilian and defense agencies. He is an adjunct professor at the Graduate School, U.S. Department of Agriculture, and George Washington University, and has authored articles in journals, including *Evaluation Review, Information Management Review*, and *Systems Management*.

STEPHEN L. DAMOURS serves as a Senior Management Analyst with the U.S. Department of State. Mr. Damours has 23 years of experience in management analysis and personnel management in federal agencies, such as, the National Institutes for Science and Technology and the Food and Drug Administration. He serves as a lecturer at the Graduate School, U.S. Department of Agriculture.

T. ARTHUR SMITH is the President of Management Analysis, Inc., a management consulting firm specializing in productivity analysis, organization restructuring, systems design and integration, and economic analysis. Dr. Smith founded MAI after completing a 25-year career with the federal government. He was Adjunct Professor of Operations Research at American University for six years.

ANDREW R. USCHER is Division Chief and Senior Management Analyst with the Office of the Secretary of Defense, Pentagon, and has 20 years of experience as a management and policy analyst. He is an Adjunct Professor at George Washington University, the author of articles in *The Bureaucrat, Military Intelligence Magazine*, and *The Armed Forces Journal*, and has served as the editor for *Management Sciences Magazine*.